HOLMES

WATSON

A MISCELLANY

S. C. ROBERTS

OTTO PENZLER BOOKS
New York

OTTO PENZLER BOOKS

Otto Penzler Books
129 West 56th Street
New York, NY 10019
(Editorial Offices only)

Simon & Schuster Inc.
Rockefeller Center
1230 Avenue of the Americas
New York, NY 10020

Reprinted by arrangement with Oxford University Press
Copyright Oxford University Press 1953

Manufactured in the United States of America

1   3   5   7   9   10   8   6   4   2

Library of Congress Cataloging-in-Publication Data
Roberts, S. C. (Sydney Castle), 1887–1966.
    Holmes & Watson: a miscellany/by S. C. Roberts.
        p.   cm.
    1. Doyle, Arthur Conan, Sir, 1859–1930—Characters—Sherlock
Holmes.   2. Doyle, Arthur Conan, Sir, 1859–1930—Characters—John H.
Watson.   3. Detective and mystery stories, English—History and criti-
cism.   4. Holmes, Sherlock (Fictitious character)   5. Watson, John H.
(Fictitious character)   6. Private investigators in literature.   7. Physicians
in literature.   I. Title.   II. Title: Holmes and Watson.
PR4624.R62   1994   94–8931   CIP
813′.54—dc20

ISBN 1-883402-96-4

PREFACE

There will be nothing original in this *Preface*. It must consist simply of two sentences stolen from the *Preface* to Monsignor R. A. Knox's *Essays in Satire* (1928):

'This book is, I am afraid, a patchwork. . . . It is a practical answer to the question, frequently asked, *Where can I get hold of that thing you wrote some years ago about Such and Such?* Well, here it is. . . .'

Such plagiarism is not, in fact, inappropriate. For it was Monsignor Knox's famous essay that first beckoned me to Baker Street.

It remains to thank those under whose auspices some portions of the patchwork have already appeared:

the Oxford University Press for the *Life* of Sherlock Holmes; Messrs. Faber & Faber for the *Life* of Dr. Watson; Messrs. Constable for the essay on Holmes's attitude to women; *The Listener* for 221B *in Retrospect*; the *Oxford Magazine* for *His music*; the *Cambridge Review* for *The Chronological Problem*; and *The Sherlock Holmes Journal* for portions of *His temperament*.

Finally, I most gratefully acknowledge the permission given for the publication of the book by the Trustees of the Estate of the late Sir Arthur Conan Doyle.

S. C. R.

CAMBRIDGE
19 *October* 1952

CONTENTS

HOLMES & WATSON

SHERLOCK HOLMES

(i) *His creation*

In the annals of publishing there are many instances of the difficult and protracted birth-pangs of what was destined to be a supremely successful book. One such example is *A Study in Scarlet*, the first recorded story of the adventures of Sherlock Holmes.

In the spring of 1886 Arthur Conan Doyle was a doctor in general practice at Southsea. But his ambitions were literary: he was already a contributor to the *Cornhill* and he had completed the draft of his first novel. He had also read Poe and Wilkie Collins and Gaboriau and his mind turned to the science, as well as to the literature, of detection. Literary influences apart, he remembered with peculiar vividness the methods of Joseph Bell, surgeon at the Edinburgh Infirmary, who had enlivened his instruction by encouraging his students to recognize a patient as a left-handed cobbler, or as a retired sergeant of a Highland regiment who had served in Barbados, by the simple processes of accurate observation and rational deduction. Into Conan Doyle's mind came the notion of a detective of highly scientific quality confronted by a murderer masquerading as a cabman, and out of this notion *A Study in Scarlet* was developed. After some experiment, the detective was named Sherlock Holmes and, with a novelist's instinct, Conan Doyle realized that his hero must have a foil and his story a narrator. Hence came the presentation of *A Study in Scarlet* as 'a reprint from the reminiscences of John H. Watson, M.D., late of the Army Medical Department' and the opening pages of the story are in fact devoted to that brief sketch of Watson's early career which was destined to form a basis of investigation for many later commentators.

Conan Doyle finished the story in April and sent it to James Payn, editor of the *Cornhill*. Payn was personally delighted with it, but returned a verdict with which all publishing houses are familiar: 'too long for a story, too short for a book'. Frederick Warne and Arrowsmith were then approached, but returned the manuscript unread. Ward Lock & Co. were slightly more responsive: they could not publish the story immediately, but if the author liked to leave it with them they would include it, with some other light pieces, in *Beeton's Christmas Annual for 1887*. So, in the year of Jubilee, the first instalment of the Reminiscences of John H. Watson, M.D., appeared, with illustrations by D. H. Friston and in company with 'two original plays for home performance'—*Food for Powder* by R. André and *The Four-leaved Shamrock* by C. J. Hamilton. *Beeton's Christmas Annual for 1887*, as is the way of Annuals, was quickly sold out and few copies were preserved. (Collectors, as Mr.

Michael Sadleir would say, will have trouble with *A Study in Scarlet*.) But, at the time, one copy was read by the editor of *Lippincott's Magazine*, who thought well enough of it to invite Conan Doyle to write another story of Sherlock Holmes. Hence came *The Sign of Four*, which was published in 1890 in both the English and American editions of *Lippincott's* and later in the same year by Spencer Blackett in book form. The book drew little attention and had to wait two years for a second edition. Today, the first edition is quoted as an example of those books 'which owe their rarity . . . to the instability of their original publishers'.

Early in 1891 Conan Doyle, who had already devoted himself to the writing of historical novels, decided finally to abandon medical work and to live by his pen. The inauguration of the *Strand Magazine* offered a suitable medium for a series of half a dozen shorter stories of Sherlock Holmes, and when *A Scandal in Bohemia* appeared in the July number of the *Strand* Holmes and Watson were quickly and firmly established in the literary tradition of the English-speaking race. These first six stories (*A Scandal in Bohemia, The Red-Headed League, A Case of Identity, The Boscombe Valley Mystery, The Five Orange Pips,* and *The Man with the Twisted Lip*) immediately captured the affection, as well as the interest, of the reading public. Furthermore, after two false starts, the iconography of Holmes and Watson was established. In the frontispiece to the original edition of *A Study in Scarlet* Holmes, though properly equipped with an Inverness cape and a magnifying glass, is represented with mutton-chop side whiskers and a nose that does not suggest the 'thin, hawk-like' quality of Watson's description; again, in the frontispiece to *The Sign of Four* (1890) Holmes, as depicted by Charles Kerr, looks like a melodramatic villain and Watson like a startled archduke. But with the first series of *Strand* stories came the invaluable co-operation of Sidney Paget as illustrator. There, at the opening of *A Scandal in Bohemia*, is the 'tall, spare figure' of Holmes standing before the Baker Street fire-place and looking down upon Watson in his 'singular introspective fashion'; there, in an interlude of the excitement of pursuing the villains of the Red-Headed League is Holmes, with lowered eyelids, seated in the stalls at St. James's Hall, enwrapped in the music of 'violin-land, where all is sweetness and delicacy and harmony and there are no red-headed clients to vex us with their conundrums'; there, on their way to unravel the Boscombe Valley mystery, are Holmes and Watson in the railway-carriage with Holmes wearing his long grey travelling-cloak and the deer-stalker cap; there, seated on a 'sort of Eastern divan', is Holmes in his blue dressing-gown at the end of the all-night sitting occasioned by the problem of the Man with the Twisted Lip, a vigil which involved the consumption of precisely one ounce of shag. These are the visual images which, perfectly harmonizing with the spirit and the atmosphere of the narrative,

combined to impart a physical realism to No. 221B
Baker Street and its famous lodgers.

Naturally, the editor of the *Strand* asked for more.
Conan Doyle was unresponsive; when pressed, he
asked for £50 a story—a price that he felt to be pro-
hibitive. But the editor knew better; he asked simply
for the quick delivery of 'copy'. So followed the second
series of six stories, from *The Blue Carbuncle* to *The
Copper Beeches*, and in 1892 the first twelve stories
were published as *The Adventures of Sherlock Holmes*.
The book was dedicated by the author to Joseph Bell
and produced in a format similar to that of the *Strand
Magazine*. Still the editor was not satisfied; again
Conan Doyle named what seemed to him a preposter-
ous sum—£1,000 for a dozen stories—and again the
fee was thankfully paid. *Silver Blaze*, the first story
of the new series, appeared in the *Strand* in December
1892 and the twelve stories were published in book
form as *The Memoirs of Sherlock Holmes* in 1894. This
time Conan Doyle really determined to make an end,
as Trollope had made an end of Mrs. Proudie—but for
an entirely different reason. It was not the readers, but
the creator, that had grown tired of Sherlock Holmes,
and in 1893 Sidney Paget was commissioned to depict
the dramatic moment at which Holmes and Moriarty,
locked in a deadly embrace, fell together into the
swirling torrent of the Reichenbach; Watson, in his
bleak loneliness, rounding off the story of the 'final
problem' with a tribute taken almost verbatim from
the last lines of the *Phaedo*.

The reading public was not only sorrowful, but furious. 'You brute', was the opening of one of the many protests addressed to the author. Conan Doyle himself had many other irons in the fire and was weary of the very name of Sherlock Holmes; but when in 1901 he listened to a friend's account of some of the legends of Dartmoor, he conceived a mystery-story about a family haunted by a spectral hound and decided to present it as an earlier adventure of the now world-famous detective. So *The Hound of the Baskervilles*, illustrated by some of Sidney Paget's best work, appeared in the *Strand* in 1901–2 and was published in book form in the latter year. Though the mortal remains of Holmes himself were still supposed to lie at the bottom of the Reichenbach Falls, the publication of this earlier adventure on Dartmoor had revived hope in the minds both of publishers and of readers, and in 1903 Conan Doyle reluctantly consented to explain how Holmes, thanks to his knowledge of baritsu, had contrived to come out alive from his duel with Moriarty. The details of this remarkable escape, as recounted by Holmes to the astonished Watson, are recorded in *The Empty House*, the adventure which inaugurated the stories grouped under the title *The Return of Sherlock Holmes* (1905). Two more collections followed—*His Last Bow* (1917) and *The Case-Book of Sherlock Holmes* (1927). Finally, the whole saga was brought together in two 'omnibus' volumes: the *Short Stories* in 1928 and the *Long Stories* in 1929.

(ii) *His life*

So much for an outline of the bibliographical history of the Adventures of Sherlock Holmes. But for the latter-day enthusiast bibliography is not enough; it is biography that he demands. 'I am lost without my Boswell', said Holmes in a famous passage and while it must be admitted that Watson's narrative cannot wholly justify the claim:

> Quo fit ut omnis
> Votiva pateat veluti descripta tabella
> Vita senis

the life and character of Sherlock Holmes can nevertheless be reconstructed with a fair measure of probability.

In his family background the two most important elements were his descent from a long line of country squires and the fact that his grandmother was a sister of Horace Vernet (1789–1863), the third of a line of French painters. Holmes's tastes and habits were, indeed, so far removed from those of the squirearchy, and Watson is so frequently at pains to emphasize the Bohemian character of life in Baker Street, that we are apt to forget how naturally and easily Holmes adapted himself to the country-house scene. With the Trevors at Donnithorpe or with the Musgraves at Hurlstone Manor or in Colonel Hayter's gun-room Holmes was completely at home; nor did he betray the slightest self-consciousness in dealing with such clients as the Duke of Holdernesse or the illustrious Lord Bellinger. But it was the Gallic side of Holmes's ancestry that more strongly influenced his way of life. 'Art in the blood', as he remarked to Watson, 'is liable to take the strangest forms' and he attributed both his own and his brother Mycroft's achievements in the art of detection to their Vernet descent. Whether, as a small boy, he ever met his great-uncle it is almost impossible to conjecture; but it is at least probable that from his early years onwards he was familiar with some of Horace Vernet's better-known pictures —for instance, with *L'Atelier d'Horace Vernet*, a graphic delineation by the artist of the motley company which gathered in his studio: 'Celui-ci, à demi couché sur une table, souffle dans un cornet à piston . . . un jeune homme lit à haute voix un journal; deux des assistants font des armes, l'un la pipe à la bouche, tenant de la main gauche une palette et un appuie-main; l'autre vêtu d'une grande blouse écrue: c'est Horace Vernet lui-même!'[1] Here, surely, is something two generations back which accords with the blue dressing-gown, the taste for fencing, the tobacco in the Persian slipper, the pistol-practice in the sitting-room, and other elements of a Bohemianism which sometimes went even beyond Watson's generous limit.

While little or nothing is known of Holmes's relations with members of his family in France or elsewhere (except, of course, for his occasional asso-

[1] C. Blanc, *Histoire des Peintres* (*École Française*), tom. iii.

ciation with Mycroft), it is noteworthy that he seldom neglected the opportunity of investigating a French problem. As early as 1886 his practice had extended to the Continent. François le Villard, a rising French detective, translated several of Holmes's pamphlets, including that on the varieties of tobacco-ash, into French and was loud in his praise of Holmes's help in a difficult will case—*magnifique, coup de maître*, he wrote in his enthusiasm. In 1887 Holmes was engaged in foiling the 'colossal schemes' of Baron Maupertuis and Watson hurried out to find him in a state of exhaustion in the Hôtel Dulong at Lyons; there followed an intricate problem at Marseilles and the case of the unfortunate Madame Montpensier, and in the winter of 1890–1 Holmes was retained by the French Government in a case of 'supreme importance'; finally, in 1894, he was responsible for bringing the Boulevard assassin, Huret, to justice—a triumph which brought him a personal letter from the President of the Republic and the Order of the Legion of Honour. It is not without significance that Holmes accepted the Order; when he was offered a knighthood in 1902, he refused it.

But, to return to the background of Holmes's upbringing, very little can be inferred about his early education. If, like Watson, he had been at one of the well-known public schools, it is difficult to believe that Watson's narrative would not have included some chance allusion to it. It is, indeed, clear that Holmes had little interest in, or knowledge of, the manly sports and exercises which delight the heart of the normal Englishman. His entire ignorance of famous rugby footballers astonished the simple soul of Cyril Overton ('sixteen stone of solid bone and muscle'), who found it hard to believe that anyone in England could be unfamiliar with the name of 'Godfrey Staunton, the crack three-quarter, Cambridge, Blackheath and five Internationals'. At the same time, Holmes admitted that amateur sport was 'the best and soundest thing in England' and he was himself a decent fencer, a good shot with a revolver, and definitely proud of his own proficiency in 'the good old British sport of boxing'.

That Holmes went to a university is, of course, quite definitely known. He told Watson that he was not a very sociable undergraduate, spending most of his time working out his own methods of thought, and that Victor Trevor was his only friend at college. The friendship was formed in a peculiar way, Trevor's bull-terrier 'freezing on' to Holmes's ankle one morning as he went down to chapel. Much legitimate, and some extravagant, inference has been drawn from this incident. Bull-terriers are not allowed within college precincts, so the attack must have occurred in the street. Therefore, it has been argued (and notably by Miss Dorothy Sayers[1]), Holmes was living out of college in his first year; and therefore, as this was a dis-

---

[1] *Baker Street Studies*, pp. 10–13. Miss Sayers's further effort to identify Sherlock Holmes with the T. S. Holmes who was admitted to Sidney Sussex College in 1871 is unfortunate. T. S. Holmes became Chancellor of Wells Cathedral.

tinctively Cambridge custom in those days, Holmes must have been at Cambridge. But the argument is not wholly conclusive; it is at least reasonable to suppose that it was a Sunday morning service to which Holmes was on his way, and he may have stepped into the street to buy a newspaper just before going to chapel. Or again, Trevor's dog may well have been tied up in the college porch, in accordance with Oxford custom.[1] Apart from this, the tone of Holmes's commentary throughout the story of *The Missing Three-Quarter* makes it impossible to believe that he was a Cambridge man. What Cambridge man talks of 'running *down* to Cambridge'? Or, again: 'Here we are, stranded and friendless, in this inhospitable town.' This, surely, is the voice of a critical stranger, not of a loyal *alumnus*. It is also relevant to recall Holmes's association with Percy (Tadpole) Phelps in the affair of *The Naval Treaty*. Phelps had been a scholar of his college at Cambridge and Holmes was brought into exceptionally close personal relationship with him; but in the course of their long talks there is not even a passing reference to Cambridge. If Holmes had, in fact, been a Cambridge man, it is difficult to believe that neither he nor Phelps should have mentioned their common Alma Mater.

The scene of *The Three Students* is laid in 'one of our great university towns'. The case involved a 'painful scandal' and Watson is at pains to conceal

---

[1] 'In the porch of the College there were, as usual, some chained-up dogs.'—Beerbohm, *Zuleika Dobson*, p. 88.

any clues by which the college of 'St. Luke's' might be identified. But it is significant that Holmes talks naturally of 'the quadrangle', a word unknown in the vocabulary of Cambridge. In *The Creeping Man* Watson, following the unfortunate lead of Dean Farrar, tantalizingly describes the university as 'Camford' and here we find Holmes affectionately reminiscent: 'There is, if I remember right, an inn called the "Chequers" where the port used to be above mediocrity, and the linen was above reproach. I think, Watson, that our lot for the next few days might lie in less pleasant places.' Here, and here alone, is the note of authenticity, and it is abundantly clear that Holmes was a 'Camford' man. 'More and more', wrote Monsignor R. A. Knox in an early treatise which has now become a classic of exploratory criticism, 'I incline to the opinion that he [Holmes] was up at the House.' It is an inclination at which no Cambridge man can cavil.

It was the father of his friend Trevor who recommended Holmes to make a profession out of what had previously been 'the merest hobby', and during the later part of his time at the university his fame spread amongst a small circle of undergraduates. Coming down from college, he took rooms in Montague Street near the British Museum and, as clients were few, he filled in time by a study of the various branches of science that were relevant to his prospective career. One of his earliest cases (*The Musgrave Ritual*), which may reasonably be dated about 1878, arose out of one of his rare undergraduate friendships, and early in

1881 came the famous meeting in the laboratory at Bart's, when young Stamford unconsciously acted as one of the great go-betweens of history and Holmes and Watson made their plans for the joint *ménage* in 221B Baker Street. In his account of the first adventure of the partnership (*A Study in Scarlet*) Watson introduces the character-sketch of his fellow lodger which must provide the basis of any biographical estimate—his late breakfasts, his alternating energy and torpor, his curious patches of ignorance (of Thomas Carlyle, for example, and of the Solar System), his violin-playing, his magazine article 'The Book of Life'. . . .

Some of Watson's early impressions naturally need qualification. As has been more than once remarked, a man who quotes Hafiz and Horace, Flaubert and Goethe, cannot fairly be described as totally ignorant of literature, and one play of Shakespeare's (*Twelfth Night*) appears to have been his particular favourite since he twice quotes a line from it in very different contexts. Holmes, indeed, was very far from being a mere calculating machine. Watson was deeply, and properly, impressed by the compilation of 'the great index volume' which served as Holmes's home-made encyclopaedia, but it was a volume which showed some curious lapses. Under the letter V, for instance, there appeared not only 'Vigor, the Hammersmith Wonder' and 'Vittoria, the circus belle' but 'Voyage of the *Gloria Scott*' and 'Victor Lynch, the forger'— exasperating entries for anyone wanting information about the *Gloria Scott* or Lynch. However, Holmes, no doubt, knew his own methods and by 1887, as has already been noted, he had become an international figure. The exceptional labours involved in the Maupertuis case had a serious effect upon his health, but he recovered in time to tackle the problem of the Reigate Squires and many others. Then came *The Sign of Four* and Watson's marriage (his first marriage) to Miss Mary Morstan. For a time the partnership was broken and it was only by hearsay that Watson knew of Holmes's summons to Odessa to investigate the Trepoff murder and of his mission on behalf of the Dutch Royal House. But the lure of 221B was strong and in 1888 the partnership was intermittently resumed, Mrs. Watson frequently encouraging her husband to respond to a tentative summons from his old friend. Thus Watson found himself engaged in the case of *The Five Orange Pips*, *The Naval Treaty*, *The Man with the Twisted Lip*, and many other famous adventures. What was described by Watson, in good faith, as *The Final Problem* belonged to the year 1891. But while Watson in the next few years was wistfully, and 'with indifferent success', attempting to apply his friend's methods to the solution of the criminal problems of the time, Holmes was in fact travelling through Tibet and other distant countries. He spent some days in Lhasa with the head Lama, then went through Persia, paid a brief visit to Mecca, and secured some useful information for the Foreign Office, probably at Mycroft's request, as the result of his interview with the Khalifa at Khartoum. Finally, he was engaged for some months in research into coal-tar derivatives in the laboratory at Montpelier. The dramatic 'Return' to Baker Street occurred in 1894, and the years that followed were busy ones indeed. Watson more than once refers to the year 1895 as 'memorable' and by the spring of 1897 the 'constant hard work' was beginning to tell upon Holmes's iron constitution. One of his last cases (*The Creeping Man*) occurred in 1903 and shortly afterwards he retired from active work and settled in Sussex. In a lonely house on the southern slope of the Downs 'commanding a great view of the Channel' the great detective lived a placid life with his housekeeper and his beehives. A great change had come over him with the passing of the years. In his record of an early adventure (*The Cardboard Box*) Watson had noted that neither sea nor country held any attraction for Holmes, but by 1907 Holmes had not only come to love the Sussex cliffs and downlands, but had convinced himself that he had always aspired after a country life, solemnly referring to 'that soothing life of Nature' as something for which he had yearned during the long years spent in London. Such is the power of Time to dull even a mind like that of Sherlock Holmes into forgetfulness—Did the ancestral squires, after all, have the last word ('naturam expellas furca, tamen usque recurret') or was it just another Gallic touch, a *Recherche du temps perdu*?

But if Holmes fell into a mood of sentimental

self-deception about his yearnings after Nature in his early days, there can be no doubt about the genuineness of his enjoyment of the Sussex Downs and the Sussex coast, especially when, after a Channel gale, all Nature was 'newly washed and fresh' and he would stroll along the cliff after breakfast and relish the 'exquisite air'. Nor was he idle. To the 'little working gangs' of bees he devoted the same intensive observation and analysis which he had before expended upon the criminal world of London, and it was with legitimate pride that he described his *Practical Handbook of Bee Culture, with some Observations upon the Segregation of the Queen* as the *magnum opus* of his later years.

About 1912 this happy absorption in apiculture was dramatically interrupted. At that time the activities of Von Bork, *facile princeps* amongst the secret agents of the Kaiser, were causing grave anxiety at Cabinet level. Strong pressure was brought upon Holmes to return to active service, and the gravity of the situation was emphasized by his receiving a visit not from an under-secretary, but from the Foreign Secretary and the Prime Minister himself. Holmes could no longer resist. He set off for Chicago, contrived to join an Irish secret society at Buffalo, and had some trouble with the police at Skibbareen. It was two years before the net was finally, and tightly, drawn and the full story of the capture of Von Bork in August 1914 is told in *His Last Bow*.

Of Holmes's way of life after 1914 no record survives. Whether he was ever again induced to emerge from his downland retreat seems doubtful. His many admirers can but await the rumoured celebration of the centenary of his birth in 1954.

(iii) *His temperament*

In the study of Holmes's personality the most insidious temptation is to seek after novelty. Like the Athenians in the time of St. Paul, Holmesian enthusiasts are always eager for some new thing. Freshness of conjecture or of conclusion is, of course, attractive; but a straining after novelty for its own sake does little to advance the purposes of sound scholarship. Still less does it accord with the principles and methods of Holmes himself, who called always for data and prescribed deduction in place of guesswork.

Of Holmes's genealogical background it has already been noted that he had a French grandmother and that his ancestors were squires who led the normal life of country gentlemen. Whether he belonged to that branch of the Holmeses which furnished two governors of the Isle of Wight in the seventeenth and eighteenth centuries who can tell? Similarly, little or nothing is known of his early upbringing. So far as his brother Mycroft is concerned, it is difficult to believe that, sixty years ago, he could have reached his unique and pivotal position in the Foreign Office if he had not had an expensive public school and university education behind him. As to Sherlock, it is, perhaps, legitimate to conjecture that, being temperamentally unfitted for the normal activities of public-school life, either he was privately educated from early boyhood or, after a short period at school, he was removed to the care of a private tutor. The nature of his physical activities certainly suggests a country house, rather than a public school, background. His ignorance of organized sport was notorious; on the other hand, such attainments as he had would naturally have been acquired at home— his tutor (or possibly one of his French kinsmen) might well have taught him to fence; from time to time, no doubt, he accompanied his father's shooting parties; and he probably learnt the elements of self-defence in friendly bouts with lads from the village.

About the Vernet influence, Holmes himself was explicit. Art was in his blood. He was not a painter, but he was passionately fond of music and he was a competent actor. Time after time he preached the doctrine of 'art for art's sake', not in any Yellow Book sense, but in a spirit of lofty altruism:

To the man who loves art for its own sake, it is frequently in its least important and lowliest manifestations that the keenest pleasure is to be derived. . . . If I claim full justice for my art, it is because it is an impersonal thing—a thing beyond myself.

Little wonder, then, that Holmes in his early days

should have rebelled against the conventions of the English squirearchy and of the English public school. Yet, as has already been noted, Watson's record of his early impressions of Holmes's unconventionality—his Bohemianism, his scorn of the softer passions, his ignorance of literature, his lack of interest in politics and philosophy—was hasty and not wholly reliable. Holmes's relations with the fair sex will be separately discussed;[1] here a word may be said about his politics.

It is, of course, true that the clash of political opinions and political parties does not seem to have aroused great interest in Holmes's mind. But, fundamentally, there can be no doubt of the breadth and liberality of his view in relation to what would now be called global politics:

I am one of those who believe that the folly of a monarch and the blundering of a Minister in far gone years will not prevent our children from being some day citizens of the same world-wide country under a flag which shall be a quartering of the Union Jack with the Stars and Stripes.

Again, it would not occur to the ordinary observer to select Clapham Junction as an inspiration of sociological optimism, but when Holmes went past it in the train, he was deeply stirred:

'Look at those big, isolated clumps of buildings rising above the slates like brick islands in a lead-coloured sea', he said to Watson.

'The Board Schools', said Watson laconically.

'Lighthouses, mv boy! Beacons of the future! Capsules,

[1] pp. 29 ff.

with hundreds of bright little seeds in each, out of which will spring the wiser, better England of the future.'

It would be difficult to find a more vivid expression of the buoyant aspirations of late Victorian Liberalism.

As to philosophy, Monsignor Knox's dogmatic assertion that 'he was not a Greats' man' must presumably be accepted. But at least he had keen anthropological interests and the problem of man's past history and of man's future destiny was constantly in his mind. In *The Sign of Four*, when he left Watson alone while he went to make some inquiries about Miss Morstan's case, he recommended him to read Winwood Reade's *The Martyrdom of Man*, describing it as one of the most remarkable works ever penned. Now *The Martyrdom of Man* was one of the most popular expositions of nineteenth-century rationalism. Holmes, with his social moodiness, his artistic temperament, and his queer intellectual interests, had no doubt reacted against the conventional beliefs of his squirearchical kinsmen and Winwood Reade's book was just the kind of work to catch him on the rebound. It is a dreary work and its conclusions may well have depressed many a contemporary of Sherlock Holmes:

A season of mental anguish is at hand and through this we must pass in order that our posterity may rise. The soul must be sacrificed; the hope in immortality must die.

It was this kind of feeling that Watson encountered in Holmes in the early years of their association and it lay at the bottom of Holmes's frequent periods of listlessness and depression. But how different was Holmes's outlook at the time of *The Veiled Lodger*, ten years after the adventure of *The Sign of Four*: 'If there is not some compensation hereafter, then the world is a cruel jest.' Again, how different were Holmes's reflections in the Phelps's garden amid the fir woods and heather of Woking. Having listened to the long and harrowing story of the loss of the Naval Treaty, he calmly held up the drooping stalk of a moss-rose and, to the astonishment of the company, delivered himself of the following meditation:

There is nothing in which deduction is so necessary as in religion. It can be built up as an exact science by the reasoner. Our highest assurance of the goodness of Providence seems to me to rest in the flowers. All other things, our powers, our desires, our food are really necessary for our existence in the first instance. But this rose is an extra. Its smell and its colour are an embellishment of life, not a condition of it. It is only goodness which gives extras. . .

Here is a passage of unusual interest which has received insufficient attention from investigators into the character of Sherlock Holmes. It suggests at least a much wider and deeper range of emotional perception than is suggested in Watson's earlier generalizations.

This is not, of course, to suggest that in his later years Holmes was moved to become a member of any organized body of religion but certainly he outgrew the cruder phases of rationalism. His profession as a criminal investigator naturally brought him face to face with what he called a circle of misery and violence and fear. 'What is the meaning of it, Watson?' he cried. 'It must lead to some end or else our universe is ruled by chance, which is unthinkable.'

Reflecting on these aspects of Holmes's personality, one cannot help thinking wistfully of those un-recorded adventures, which have taken the place of the lost books of Livy in the modern world, and, in particular, of those cases undertaken at the request of the Pope. Recently I had the tantalizingly good fortune to come upon two fragments of an imperfect Watson manuscript. They must, I think, be portions of a rough draft of *The Death of Cardinal Tosca* and are appended here for what they are worth:

In the course of my long association with my friend Sherlock Holmes it was only occasionally that I heard him refer to the great questions underlying the creeds and dogmas of the religions of the world. I knew that the rule of the universe by chance was to his mind unthinkable, but in the religious organisations of the civilised world, as such, he seldom displayed an interest.

I had, on a particular morning, come down to breakfast rather late. Holmes, not being engaged in any investiga-tion at the time, sat moodily silent in his arm-chair, blow-ing thick clouds of tobacco smoke across the room. I, equally silent, poured out my coffee and read *The Daily Telegraph*. In about five minutes the silence was broken and, to my surprise, by Holmes.

'Yes, I agree, Watson. It must be a wonderful thing to be a convinced member of the Catholic Church.'

'My dear Holmes, what are you talking about?'

'About the same thing that you are thinking about.'

'But, Holmes, this is ridiculous. I have done nothing but read the morning paper.'

'Precisely, my dear Watson. The morning paper, which I studied before you were out of bed, is unusually dull today, except for the news in the fourth column of the right-hand middle page upon which I observed your eyes to be concentrated until a minute ago. Then you looked up thoughtfully, your hand went to the lower right-hand pocket of your waistcoat where you no doubt felt the little cross on the end of your watch-chain, a legacy from your devout mother—a simple little action, from which I made the equally simple deduction that after reading of the dramatic death of Cardinal Tosca yesterday, you reflected for a moment, as I had done, upon what it must mean to belong to that remarkable institution, the Catholic Church.'

'You're perfectly right, Holmes,' I replied, 'and it is difficult to imagine death coming in a more sublime form than that in which it overtook the Cardinal.'

'I wonder,' said Holmes laconically.

'Oh, of course, you and I and the great majority of Englishmen are outsiders in this matter, but here was this old man, with a long and honourable career behind him and in the act of performing one of the sacred duties of his office, passing swiftly and painlessly to that other world on which his affections were set.'

'Watson, you are an incurable romantic. How do you know that the poor Cardinal's death was painless? What do you know of the other-worldliness of his interests?'

'Oh, come, Holmes. I only know what I have read in the paper. Listen: "Seldom has the hand of Death fallen more suddenly or more dramatically than it fell yesterday upon the revered figure of Cardinal Tosca. The Cardinal who had arrived in England in the early part of last week was the guest of the well-known preacher, Father Cuthbert

Jameson, and had undertaken to officiate at the service of
Benediction at the Church of the Immaculate Conception
in Knightsbridge. The Cardinal who was in his 68th year
and appeared to be in excellent health was about to offer
the prayer of humble adoration when he suddenly col-
lapsed. He was reverently carried by a willing band of
worshippers to the church door and was conveyed in the
charge of his faithful body-servant to Father Jameson's
house in Bayswater. At first it was hoped that the seizure
might be of a temporary nature, but the Cardinal never
recovered consciousness." '

'Well?' said Holmes.

'Well,' I replied, 'a very tragic, but a very beautiful,
death.'

'Tragic certainly, my dear Watson, but as to the beauty
of it—well, while you were shaving—by the way, Watson,
you cut your strop rather badly this morning, didn't you?'

'I did, Holmes, but how on earth d'you know that?'

'Oh, a trifle. I listen every morning to the rhythm of
your admirably even movements. This morning there was
a sudden, harsh sound followed by a pause. Then the
stropping began again, but the strokes were shorter—
clearly you had put about one-third of your strop out of
action.'

'Quite right, Holmes, but—'

'Well, what I was about to suggest was that there may
have been elements other than beauty in the Cardinal's
death.'

'D'you mean that you suspect foul play?'

'I suspect nothing, Watson, I have no data—with the
exception of a few details of the Cardinal's career which I
found in my Index—under C. But whether they are relevant, who can tell?' Holmes said no more and gazed
moodily out of the window. Suddenly he became alert.

'Why, what's this?' he exclaimed. 'Here's my brother Mycroft coming to see me and hurrying too. Ah, there must be something interesting afoot. It's no ordinary business that makes brother Mycroft quicken his steps at this hour of the morning.'

In a few minutes the massive figure of Mycroft Holmes entered the room.

'Sherlock,' he said curtly, 'I want your help.'

'You mean that someone else wants it, Mycroft. You wouldn't expend this unusual energy on your own behalf.'

'Quite right, Sherlock. I've been intolerably pressed ever since I got up this morning. First, a special messenger telling me to report immediately to the Foreign Office. Then a hasty interview with the Permanent Under Secretary, who informed me that the Minister had received a personal request to make immediate investigation into the death of Cardinal Tosca.'

'From Rome?' asked Sherlock.

'Yes, the Pope himself is extremely anxious for a detailed enquiry and requested that your services should be employed.' Holmes's eyes twinkled. As he had told me years before, he never reckoned modesty amongst his virtues.

'There's fame for you, Watson,' he said.

'Yes, Dr. Watson,' said Mycroft. 'But please pity the poor brother of the investigator your chronicles have made famous.'

Before I could answer, Sherlock broke in:

'But what did His Holiness tell you about the Cardinal? What data have you brought, Mycroft?'

'Practically nothing, Sherlock. You know what's in the papers, I expect. I don't. I don't read newspapers. All I have is a little collection of facts about the Cardinal taken from the Foreign Office dossier.'

He handed a piece of paper to his brother. Sherlock scanned it eagerly.

'Ah,' he said, 'a few new items, but not much more than I have on my own files.'

'Well,' said Mycroft, 'my part is done. I don't often cadge a drink, Sherlock, but I had an abominably hasty breakfast this morning. Have you any coffee left?'

I was in the act of pouring out a cup for the exhausted Mycroft, when Sherlock, who was once more looking out of the window, remarked:

'I believe we're to have another visitor. Come and look, Mycroft. He's in a hurry, as you were—clearly a domestic servant.'

'Obviously,' said Mycroft lazily, 'also a Roman Catholic.'

'By jove, Mycroft, you're right. This begins to be exciting.'

'Holmes,' I said, 'what is all this about?'

'Only, my dear Watson, that as usual, Mycroft's process of observation is quicker than mine. The cut of the man's black coat indicated the manservant at once, but I was slower than my brother to notice the pendant on his watch chain.'

By this time we heard hurried steps in the passage and our visitor entered. He was a smooth-faced, deferential little man, but obviously in a state of agitation.

'Oh, which of you gentlemen is Mr. Sherlock Holmes, please?' he gasped.

Sherlock stepped forward and begged the little man to sit down. 'Here I am,' he said, 'with Mr. Mycroft Holmes, my brother, and Dr. Watson, my colleague—now tell us your story.'

'Well, sir,' our visitor began, 'my name is Goodwin—Joseph Sebastian Goodwin and I'm confidential servant to Father Jameson. Of course you've heard, sir, of this terrible affair of Cardinal Tosca.'

'Yes, indeed,' said Sherlock Holmes. 'But we want to hear a great deal more about it than what is in the papers. Now you are the very man to tell us quietly just what happened.'

'Quietly?' said Goodwin. 'How can I tell you quietly when the *body's gone?*'

Even Mycroft was startled and spilled some coffee down his ample waistcoat—but he quickly recovered.

'Anything else gone with it?' he asked.

'I don't understand you, sir,' said Goodwin.

'Don't try,' replied Mycroft, 'I have no business to be asking questions, but I daresay you'll find my brother even more inquisitive.'

'And now,' he went on, turning to Sherlock, 'I must go back to my office. Good-bye, Sherlock, thank you for the coffee. I'm glad to see that you've already collected a few data. If you want me later in the day, you'll find me at the Diogenes. . . .

* * * * *

When we were comfortably settled in the railway-carriage at Lime Street, I ventured to ask Holmes what had given him his first clue.

'My dear Watson,' he replied, 'I must again remind you of Mycroft's extraordinary quickness. When he asked that little man Goodwin whether anything besides the body had disappeared, I saw at once what was in his mind. When, later, Goodwin remarked that the Cardinal's servant was wearing a different suit of clothes on the morning after the disappearance, my suspicions were confirmed. What use had been made of the first suit of clothes? It was true, of course, that the Cardinal was unconscious when he was carried out of church. But, as you yourself pertinently observed, there was no medical certificate of death. I needn't weary you with all the links in the chain of evidence, but having once adopted the hypothesis that the Cardinal was still alive, I found that everything seemed to fit—or at least that nothing seemed to conflict with it. One serious gap in my knowledge was the very scant information in my index about the Cardinal's early life. But a telegraphed enquiry to an old friend of mine in the Rome police brought an answer showing that the Cardinal had in early youth belonged for a very short time to a Neapolitan Society suspected to be anarchistic and anti-clerical in character— the sort of brotherhood that never forgives a deserter. So when I came upon that letter with the kind of cryptic threat which we have encountered in other cases, I felt fairly confident that the Cardinal had borrowed a suit of clothes and made off.'

'But how did you know he'd sail from Liverpool?'

'I didn't know, Watson. But he would naturally be anxious to get out of England and out of Europe. Clearly he would go west and Liverpool seemed to me more prob- able than Southampton. Well, the good Cardinal is now on his way to Quebec where he has many friends; and we, if this train is punctual, shall just be in time for a meal at Simpson's and some soothing music at the Albert Hall.'

(iv) *His attitude to women*

Certain imaginative playwrights, with a greater regard for popular sentiment than for documentary evidence, have boldly portrayed Sherlock Holmes not only as a lover, but as husband and father. To the ordinary playgoer such conjectural creations may afford a pleasant evening's entertainment; but, in the eyes of serious students of the literature of Baker

Street, they are a wholly unworthy tribute to the man who cried 'Give me data'; furthermore they tend to obscure the more pressing problems of Holmesian scholarship.

At the same time a careful re-examination of the whole question of Holmes's attitude towards the fair sex may well be regarded as one of the major *desiderata*. Granted the unreality which must characterize any picture of Holmes in the conventional bliss of domesticity, have not scholars in the past been too prone to uncritical acceptance of Holmes as misogynist? For this view Watson himself is, no doubt, principally responsible. Having stated categorically in *The Sign of Four* the grounds of Holmes's objections to matrimony ('Love is an emotional thing . . . opposed to that true, cold reason which I place above all things. I should never marry myself, lest I bias my judgement'), he proceeds in *A Scandal in Bohemia* to elaborate his theme:

It was not that he felt any emotion akin to love for Irene Adler. All emotions, and that one particularly, were abhorrent to his cold, precise, but admirably balanced mind. He was, I take it, the most perfect reasoning and observing machine that the world has seen: but, as a lover, he would have placed himself in a false position. He never spoke of the softer passions, save with a gibe and a sneer. They were admirable things for the observer—excellent for drawing the veil from men's motives and actions. But for the trained reasoner to admit such intrusions into his own delicate and finely adjusted temperament was to introduce a distracting factor which might throw a doubt upon all his mental results. Grit in a sensitive instrument, or a crack in one of his own high-power lenses, would not be more disturbing than a strong emotion in a nature such as his.

It is noteworthy that this characterization belongs to a period in which Watson was absorbed in the new-found happiness of his own first marriage, the happiness which lies in the 'home-centred interests which rise up around the man who first finds himself master of his own establishment'. At such a time Holmes appeared to him as one who 'loathed every form of society with his whole Bohemian soul', and it was inevitable that Watson, the literary artist, should heighten the contrast. But Watson's artistry must not be allowed to mislead us. We must look upon other pictures of Holmes than these impressionist sketches of Holmes the Confirmed Misogynist and Holmes the Complete Bohemian. Before a true judgement upon Holmes's relations with women can properly be passed, it is necessary to review a larger body of evidence and to review it in such a spirit of scientific detachment as Holmes himself would have approved.

It is, of course, true that Holmes was 'never a very sociable fellow'. Victor Trevor was the only friend he made at college, but he was a 'close friend' and a real 'bond of union' was formed between them. The nature of the common ground on which they met is also worth remark: 'He [Trevor] was as friendless as I,'[1] Holmes rather wistfully records. May not

[1] *The 'Gloria Scott'*.

Holmes have belonged to that class of persons—a class larger than is commonly realized—who fervently and secretly rejoice in congenial society, but are debarred by deep-seated inhibitions from making the initiatory step in a social rapprochement? To the peculiar significance of Holmes's further relations with Trevor we shall return later. For the moment it may be worth while to recall Holmes's eagerness to secure a fellow-lodger in No. 221B Baker Street. It is true that the recorded motive is a financial one, but no one fundamentally unsociable would have taken the risk, especially with a complete stranger, of setting up a joint establishment. Clearly, Holmes was glad of company, even before the development of his personal affection for Watson himself. In the early days, to put the case at its lowest, Watson's company was a solace when clients were few and far between. Holmes abominated the 'dull routine of existence'; he craved for 'mental exaltation' and this exaltation could only come from the study of his fellow human beings. For it would be a mistake to regard Holmes as being devoted to scientific investigation for its own sake. To him the laboratory was a means, not an end. His famous discovery of a reagent precipitated exclusively by hæmoglobin thrilled him not as an addition to chemical knowledge, but as 'the most practical medico-legal discovery for years.'[1] When he had no case in hand, Holmes, so far from filling his leisure happily with

---

[1] *A Study in Scarlet.*

independent laboratory research, was obliged, much to Watson's distress, to have recourse to artificial stimulants. While he might, in the Johnsonian sense, have been described as an 'unclubable' man, he was, nevertheless, as incapable of supporting a mental solitude as Johnson himself. Like Johnson,[1] he was, in his own way, obliged to anyone who visited him. If no clients rang the bell of No. 221B Baker Street, Holmes would console himself with his Boswell, whom he admitted to be indispensable.

So much, then, may be said by way of introduction and by way of dispelling the notion that Holmes was by nature a recluse. Of his attitude towards women in particular we have, fortunately, a very considerable body of evidence.

Among the early adventures none stands out more clearly than *The Speckled Band*. At the outset Holmes greets Miss Stoner with a cheerfulness which betokens his satisfaction at the initiation of a new problem. Watson is introduced and hot coffee is ordered for the lady. But it was no time for the 'exchange of social pleasantries'.

'It is not cold which makes me shiver,' said the woman in a low voice, changing her seat as requested.

'What then?'

'It is fear, Mr. Holmes. It is terror.'

At once Holmes's manner changes:

'You must not fear,' he says soothingly, and bending forward he pats the poor girl's forearm.

[1] See pp. 52 ff.

Little wonder that Miss Stoner's heart was lightened when she left Baker Street. Holmes's sympathy had been of no merely formal kind—he had pressed her to stay to breakfast. The affair of the Speckled Band was, as Watson quickly deduced, 'a most dark and sinister business'. At Stoke Moran Holmes's protectiveness in regard to Miss Stoner is again evident. Naturally the poor girl was overjoyed to see her friends. Quickly she began to follow the working of Holmes's mind: 'I believe, Mr. Holmes, that you have already made up your mind.' Further, she was not afraid to lay her hand upon the detective's sleeve. 'Good-bye and be brave,' was Holmes's parting injunction as, with Watson by his side, he left Miss Stoner on the fateful night when Dr. Grimesby Roylott's villainies met with their most fitting punishment; finally, Holmes accompanied Watson in breaking the news to the terrified girl and in conveying her to the care of her good aunt of Harrow.

In *A Case of Identity*, again, Miss Mary Sutherland's troubles aroused, in the first instance, little more than a professional interest in Holmes's mind. 'Oscillation upon the pavement,' he told the wondering Watson, 'always means an *affaire du cœur*. . . . When a woman has been seriously wronged by a man she no longer oscillates, and the usual symptom is a broken bell wire.'

Miss Sutherland enters the room. Holmes greets her with the 'easy courtesy' of the professional consultant. But as her story is unfolded, he displays a

warmth of feeling far beyond the limits of dispassion-
ate inquiry. 'You have been very shamefully treated,'
he cries at one point, and the advice he gives her at
the conclusion of the interview has reference to the
girl's own peace of mind rather than to the problem
of the missing bridegroom. As he frankly confessed
to Watson, he found the girl more interesting than
the case. The case, indeed, held little of novelty or
attraction for Holmes; he had come across similar
affairs at Andover and at The Hague. It was Mary
Sutherland who engrossed his attention, and, later,
it was no mere passion for justice in the abstract, but
the throbbing pulse of human sympathy that made
him long to lay a horsewhip across the shoulders of
the scoundrelly James Windibank. Holmes's final
comment on the case reveals a profundity of insight
into feminine psychology:

'If I tell her she will not believe me. You may
remember the old Persian saying, "There is danger
for him who taketh the tiger cub, and danger also for
whoso snatches a delusion from a woman."'

It was a maxim that was later to receive a terrible
confirmation in the case of *The Illustrious Client*.

Evidences of the affectionate feelings which Holmes
entertained from time to time towards his lady clients
peep out from Watson's narrative. It is to Watson,
of course, that we normally owe the more detailed
descriptions of feminine dress and appearance. Mrs.
St. Clair, for instance, was 'a little blonde woman . . .
clad in some sort of light *mousseline-de-soie*, with a

touch of fluffy pink chiffon at her neck and wrists. She stood', Watson continues, 'with her figure outlined against the flood of light, one hand upon the door, one half raised in eagerness, her body slightly bent, her head and face protruded, with eager eyes and parted lips, a standing question.'

A careless reading of *The Man with the Twisted Lip* might suggest that such a vision had no effect upon the apostle of 'true, cold reason'. But it was Holmes who confessed: 'I was wondering what I should say to this dear little woman to-night'; it was Holmes who told Neville St. Clair that he would have done better to have trusted his wife.

Instinctively Holmes was quick to grasp the woman's point of view, as the unfortunate Lord Robert St. Simon[1] discovered. Holmes, indeed, could 'hardly see how the lady could have acted otherwise' than vanish at the wedding breakfast. She was, as he said, motherless and had no one to advise her in a crisis.

'It was a slight, sir, a public slight,' protested the noble bachelor.

'You must make allowance for this poor girl,' was Holmes's reply, and the supper ordered from outside to do honour to the lady was of a quality unprecedented in the annals of 221B Baker Street.[2]

Once, when Holmes received a request for advice

---

[1] Holmes's repeated reference to 'Lord St. Simon' is a curious solecism; it may perhaps be due to carelessness on Watson's part when he put his notes into narrative form.

[2] 'A couple of brace of cold woodcock, a pheasant, a *pâté-de-foie-gras* pie, with a group of ancient and cobwebby bottles.'

about the offer of a post as governess, he petulantly
complained of the triviality of the application:

'As to my own little practice,' he broke out to
Watson, 'it seems to be degenerating into an agency
for recovering lost lead pencils and giving advice to
young ladies from boarding-schools. I think that I
have touched bottom at last. . . .'[1]

But when Miss Violet Hunter ('with a bright quick
face freckled like a plover's egg' as Watson vividly
describes her) appeared at Baker Street in person, it
was at once apparent that Holmes was favourably
impressed. Later, when Miss Hunter's story of her
experience at the Copper Beeches had been told,
Holmes was moved to warm and unstinted praise:
'You seem to me,' he declared, 'to have acted all
through this matter like a brave and sensible girl.'
So marked, indeed, was Holmes's admiration that
Watson expresses his disappointment that Holmes
should have manifested no further interest in the girl
after they had safely conducted her to Winchester.
Why should Watson be disappointed? It cannot,
surely, have been on his own account.[2] He was a
married man at the time, and, though his wife's
health was probably failing, it is not to be imagined
that he had taken anything more than a comradely
interest in Violet Hunter. Why, then, if we are to
accept Watson's own picture of his friend as 'loath-
ing every form of society with his whole Bohemian

[1] *The Copper Beeches.*
[2] In this connexion I cannot accept H. W. Bell's inferences (*Sherlock Holmes and Dr. Watson*, p. 68).

soul', should he be surprised at Holmes losing interest in the lady as soon as her problem had been solved? We are driven to conclude that Watson had been so strongly impressed by Holmes's unusually warm regard for Miss Hunter that he hoped that the friendship might ripen and develop.[1]

Harshness, as Watson says, was foreign to Holmes's nature, and when a 'young and beautiful woman, tall, graceful, and queenly'[2] broke in upon the investigation of the abstruse and complicated problem of John Vincent Harden, the tobacco magnate, Holmes, a little put out at first, begged the beautiful intruder to take a seat. As the lady's story was unfolded, he quickly grew sympathetic.

'Oh, Cyril is his name!' he broke in archly at one point; and when Violet Smith had gone, he had no doubt about her charm: 'It is part of the settled order of Nature that such a girl should have followers', he said, pulling at a meditative pipe. For a time he was uncertain whether Miss Smith's troubles would prove to be anything more than a trivial affair, but after a fuller investigation he quickly changed his view: 'It is our duty', he told Watson, 'to see that no one molests her upon that last journey.' Just as Holmes was constantly moved to compassionate as well as professional interest by the distress of a defenceless girl, so he showed an extreme warmth, as well as a nice delicacy, of feeling in regard to any disaster

[1] Miss Hunter became head of a school at Walsall. It is possible that the whole Birmingham area held a measure of poignancy for Holmes (see below, pp. 42, 43). [2] *The Solitary Cyclist.*

which might threaten to wreck a happy marriage. The dialogue between him and the unfortunate Lady Hilda Trelawney Hope is one of the most dramatic in the whole series of adventures.

'She stood grandly defiant,' writes Watson, 'a queenly figure, her eyes fixed upon his as if she would read his very soul.' But the defiance could not last and before long she was at Holmes's feet, 'her beautiful face upturned and wet with her tears.' Gently raising her, he uttered no word of reproach, but quietly expressed his thankfulness for her eleventh-hour confession. All her defences down, the lady told her whole story: 'Put yourself in my position, Mr. Holmes! What was I to do?' The reply was the same as the advice given to Neville St. Clair: 'Take your husband into your confidence. . . .' Holmes's satisfaction in protecting Lady Hilda's secret was evident. 'We also have our diplomatic secrets', he told the Prime Minister.[1]

But nowhere is the depth of Holmes's feeling for the sanctity of feminine beauty and innocence more eloquently revealed than in the famous story of *The Illustrious Client*:

'I don't quite know how to make her [Violet de Merville] clear to you, Watson. Perhaps you may meet her before we are through, and you can use your own gift of words. She is beautiful, but with the ethereal other-world beauty of some fanatic whose thoughts are set on high. I have seen such faces in the pictures of the old masters of the Middle Ages.'

[1] *The Second Stain*

In vain he pleaded with her as he would have pleaded with a daughter of his own. The occasion spurred him to unwonted eloquence. Emotion triumphed over intellect, and every degree of warmth of which he was capable was concentrated in his appeal:

'I pictured to her,' as he told Watson, 'the awful position of the woman who only wakes to a man's character after she is his wife—a woman who has to submit to be caressed by bloody hands and lecherous lips. . . .'

Seldom indeed was Holmes keyed to so melodramatic a pitch; and it was only the spectacle of a wronged and beautiful woman that could so move him.[1]

The same feeling is manifested in the well-known story of *Charles Augustus Milverton*, and there are few more tender passages in the literature of Baker Street than that at the conclusion of *The Veiled Lodger*, when Holmes was impelled to make one of his rare comments on the riddle of the universe: 'Poor girl!' he cried. 'The ways of Fate are indeed hard to understand. If there is not some compensation hereafter, then the world is a cruel jest.' With his quick

---

[1] Elsewhere, pp. 89, 90, I have suggested that Miss de Merville afterwards became the second wife of Dr. Watson. Critics have dismissed this theory as fantastic or even as negligible, sometimes with a greater measure of scorn than of argument. The objection that Watson would not have cared to record his wife's early misfortunes is certainly valid, but it should be remembered (*a*) that the story was not published for twenty years after the events described; (*b*) that Watson may have disguised the surnames in his narrative. If my theory is correct, it may well be that the unusually fervid description owes something to Watson's own feelings.

intuition, he observed something significant in the voice of Eugenia Ronder as she came to the end of her tragic story:

'Your life is not your own,' he said. 'Keep your hands off it.'

'What use is it to anyone?'

'How can you tell? The example of patient suffering is in itself the most precious of all lessons to an impatient world.'

As is well known, Holmes's solemn injunction had its effect. The brave woman ('the poor wounded beast that had crawled into its hole to die') took the detective's counsel and with it fresh courage.

Such examples as these—and doubtless they could be supplemented—of Holmes's tenderness and sensibility in his relations with women are surely of some significance. At the very least their cumulative effect is to dispel the common impression that Holmes was a misogynist or that women only interested him as 'cases'. Of course, like any specialist, Holmes approached his clients in the first instance from a purely professional angle, but again and again we have evidence that this professional interest was supplemented and intensified by a quick and intuitive sympathy evoked, more often than not, by the tale of a woman's distress. When his heart was thus touched, he did not, except in rare cases, elaborate the theme in conversation with Watson. Watson, indeed, was no doubt misled, as many of his readers have been misled, by the measure of Holmes's more expansive comment on Irene Adler. 'To Sherlock Holmes she was always *the* woman.' But this is a purely intellectual tribute—an outburst of admiration for the woman who outwitted him. To the scale of Holmes's emotional values it has no kind of relevance.

If, then, we are right in crediting Holmes with a more lively understanding of the feminine point of view than has been heretofore assumed, are there elements in the background of his life which would tend to substantiate this fresh conception of the great detective's emotional make-up? It must be admitted at once that the material is slight. Of Holmes's relations the only one definitely known to us is Mycroft; as we have already noted, his ancestors were country squires of orthodox habits; one of his grandmothers was French and the sister of an artist. As an undergraduate he had only one intimate friend—Victor Trevor. Now when Trevor invited Holmes to his father's country house in Norfolk, Holmes appears to have accepted the invitation with alacrity, and he stayed not a week-end, but a month. There was good fishing and duck-shooting, a good library and good food, and Holmes makes no disguise of the fact that life was pleasant at Donnithorpe. He proceeds to explain that Victor Trevor was an only son, that his father was a widower and that his sister was dead: 'There had been a daughter, I heard, but she had died of diphtheria while on a visit to Birmingham.' This is a curious sentence. The fact of Trevor senior's (*alias* James Armitage) having had a daughter as well as a son has little or no relevance to the story of the *Gloria Scott*. That Holmes should mention the daughter in describing the Donnithorpe household to Watson is, perhaps, natural enough. But why should he particularize both the nature and the occasion of her death? 'She had died of diphtheria while on a visit to Birmingham.' Why—one is bound to press the question—did Holmes suddenly recall the circumstantial and, on the face of it, second-hand details about the decease of his friend's sister? But were they, in fact, second-hand? Is it possible that Holmes's pluperfect is just an emotional camouflage? It will be remembered that after his father's death Victor Trevor went out to be a tea-planter in the Terai and that Holmes kept in touch with him. Assuming, for the moment, that Trevor's sister was in fact alive at the time of her father's tragic death, she would naturally spend some time after the melancholy event among friends or relations. Assuming, further, that Holmes's specific, and yet wholly superfluous reference, conceals an indication of some closer interest than is conveyed in the bald sentence in the narrative of *The 'Gloria Scott'*,[1] are we not justified in the conjecture, to put it no higher, that Holmes was in fact attracted to Miss Trevor and that his

[1] The late H. W. Bell (*Sherlock Holmes and Dr. Watson*, pp. 7 ff.) pointed out a number of inconsistencies in the story of James Armitage and concluded either that Holmes was too young and impressionable to subject it to critical analysis or that 'in a freakish mood' he concocted the story himself. It would appear more likely that Holmes deliberately varied certain parts of the whole narrative in order to conceal its importance in his own emotional history.

hopes and affections were rudely shattered by the ravages of diphtheria in Birmingham in the seventies?[1]

It is not difficult to imagine how, after such an annihilation of his early hopes, Holmes would for the time renounce the whole race of women except in so far as they might be of promise, or of service, in the profession of scientific detection. His was just such a nature as would, after a severe disappointment in youth, react violently from the cultivation of female society. Here may be found the true explanation of the elevation of the 'true, cold reason' which Holmes placed above all things. It is the typical reaction, familiar to all psychologists, of frustrated desire. Further, it seems extremely probable that one of the more tragic symptoms of this reaction is to be found in the cocaine habit, which was an object of very natural distress to Watson. Here it is worth while recalling some passages in the well-known dialogue at the end of *The Sign of Four*. When Watson announced his engagement, Holmes gave a most dismal groan and refused to congratulate his friend. Naturally Watson was a little hurt. Had Holmes anything against the lady?

'Not at all', was the reply. 'I think she is one of the most charming young ladies I ever met. . . .' Watson was relieved, but noted that Holmes looked weary. Yes, Holmes admitted, the reaction was already upon him; there came over him, too, the wistful dualism of Goethe. Why had Nature made but *one* man out

[1] The average death-rate per 1,000 of the population from diphtheria in the seventies was 0·43 as compared with 0·03 in 1932. (Information kindly supplied by the Medical Officer of Health of Birmingham.)

of the stuff whereof he himself was fashioned? He could, he reflected, have been a 'pretty spry sort of fellow'. Finally the good-hearted Watson declared:

'The division seems rather unfair. You have done all the work in this business. I get a wife out of it, Jones gets the credit; pray what remains for you?'

'For me,' said Sherlock Holmes, 'there remains the cocaine-bottle.' If we are justified in our conjecture concerning Holmes's previous history,[1] does not this whole passage assume a new sadness and a new significance?

'Work', as Holmes himself remarked to Watson on a later occasion, 'is the best antidote to sorrow';[2] and with the passing of years it is noteworthy that we read less about cocaine and more about the geniality, and even tenderness, of Holmes's relations with the fair sex.[3]

In the quest of the whole truth of the inner history of Sherlock Holmes the thesis presented here cannot claim to be more than an essay in exploration; but one thing is certain: Holmes cannot, on a proper examination of the evidence, be any longer regarded as the embodiment of asexual ratiocination.

[1] Holmes was a good actor, and it would be unfair to adduce his engagement to Milverton's housemaid as important evidence; but it may be remarked that he appears to have played his part with a total lack of embarrassment.

[2] *The Empty House.*

[3] It would be interesting to discover the Christian name of Victor Trevor's sister. I conjecture that it was Violet. It is noteworthy that this name belonged to three ladies (Miss Hunter, Miss Smith, and Miss de Merville) whom Holmes treated with more than ordinary courtesy.

(v) *His music*[1]

Mr. Warrack makes his entry into the field of Holmesian scholarship with disarming modesty. But let it be said at once that he fully justifies his admission to the company of serious investigators of the problems of 221B Baker Street. A careful examination of Holmes's musical tastes and accomplishments has long been a desideratum amongst students of the Watson Saga, and Mr. Warrack's well-documented monograph, save for a few regrettable lapses, preserves the true spirit of patient scholarship. His investigation, for instance, of the circumstances under which Sherlock Holmes bought his Stradivari from a Jew broker in the Tottenham Court Road for fifty-five shillings is a masterly piece of reconstruction. Mr. Warrack is able to show that in 1872, just at the time when Holmes might be spending part of his vacation in London, there was a Special Loan exhibition of musical instruments at South Kensington, and that at the same time a series of letters on Cremona Violins and Varnish was appearing in the *Pall Mall Gazette*. In the same year, too, Lombardini's *Antonio Stradivari e la celebre scuola cremonese* was published, and Mr. Warrack's researches throw a bright and convincing light on what was undoubtedly Holmes's favourite recreation.

Mr. Warrack's survey includes a similarly learned commentary upon Holmes's study of 'The Poly-

[1] A review of Guy Warrack, *Sherlock Holmes and Music* (1947).

phonic Motets of Lassus'. All readers of *The Bruce-Partington Plans* will remember that it was in 1895 that Holmes undertook the writing of a monograph on this subject; that it was afterwards printed for private circulation, and that, according to Watson, it was 'said by experts to be the last word on the subject'. Mr. Warrack approaches this topic in a highly sceptical spirit: he is doubtful whether Holmes ever heard much of Lassus's music sung, and is probably right in inferring that his study of it must have been from the printed page. But with Mr. Warrack's conclusion that the monograph was 'at best only projected, at the worst a complete myth', we find ourselves unable to agree. Certainly Watson's remark about its being 'the last word' is merely a hearsay quotation, but such slight evidence as we have of the nature of Holmes's work by no means rules out the possibility of its having dealt minutely with some aspect—possibly the bibliographical aspect—of Lassus's work. With his French connexions and with his well-known interest in typographical technique, Holmes may well have developed an enthusiasm for the study of the early editions published in Paris by Le Roy side by side with the later Ballard editions, and so have thrown fresh light on certain points of musical typography. Here, admittedly, we are in the realm of musicological conjecture, but we feel bound to prefer conjecture, however tentative, to the sweeping nature of Mr. Warrack's *non est inventus* conclusion.

Again, we cannot wholly accept Mr. Warrack's

destructive analysis of the gramophone incident in *The Mazarin Stone*. Holmes, it will be remembered, utilizes the newly invented gramophone to play the Barcarolle from Offenbach's *Contes d'Hoffmann*, and Mr. Warrack seeks to cast doubt upon the whole episode, suggesting that the gramophone is, in fact, an editorial invention. Now it may be conceded at once that the text of *The Mazarin Stone* presents many difficulties. It does not form part of the Watson canon, and Holmes is made to split an infinitive at the climax of the adventure; elsewhere[1] we have ventured to make a conjecture as to the probable editorship of the story, and we cannot but be gratified that Mr. Warrack has thought fit to adopt this conjecture. But in his discussion of the problem from the angle of the Barcarolle itself we are compelled to doubt whether he has preserved a proper objectivity of approach. Mr. Warrack, as he informs us in a modest footnote, was an Examiner for the Associated Board of the Royal Schools of Music for many years, and it is with real diffidence that we would venture any criticism of his purely musical exegesis. But when he writes of the Barcarolle that 'Many musicians consider it to be a particularly feeble and dreary tune justified only by its operatic setting', it is only fair to reply that there are musicians of distinction who would resent with some warmth this attribution of dreary feebleness. Further, when Mr. Warrack goes on: 'Played on a solo violin it is intolerable, as indeed

[1] p. 91 n.

Count Negretto Silvius found', we become less and less confident of his critical impartiality. For, in supporting his argument, he quotes the Count (whose name, incidentally, is misspelt) as saying: 'Confound that whining noise; it gets on my nerves.' What the Count actually said was: 'Confound that whining music. . . .' No less an authority than Grove is quoted for the view that the popularity of the Barcarolle dates from Sir Thomas Beecham's English production of the opera in 1910, and *The Mazarin Stone* must certainly be dated 1903, or 1904 at the latest. But what Mr. Warrack would seem to have overlooked is that the Barcarolle was largely popularized in this country as a dance-tune. In the early 1900s it was well established as a favourite waltz, especially as played by the first violin of a small dance-orchestra; and, while Mr. Warrack's doubt about the existence of a gramophone record in 1903 is fully justified, it may be noted that, in the early days of gramophone development, 'vocal and violin solos made the most successful records'.[1] In short, the proper approach to a history of the Barcarolle is to be sought not in the annals of the Opéra Comique, but on the Edvardian dancing-floor.

Finally, a word must be said upon Mr. Warrack's attitude towards Holmes himself. It savours, we regret to say, both of patronage and of denigration. We may pass by the suggestion that a fondness for Mendelssohn, Meyerbeer, and Offenbach indicates

[1] *Oxford Companion to Music* (1938), p. 378.

that Holmes had Jewish blood in his veins as a piece of ill-judged pleasantry. But Holmes's 'propensity for ostentation' and his 'love of a good curtain' seem to rouse in Mr. Warrack a disproportionate degree of critical irritation. The opening pages of *Silver Blaze* are well known:

'We are going well,' said he, looking out of the window, and glancing at his watch. 'Our rate at present is fifty-three and a half miles an hour.'

'I have not observed the quarter-mile posts,' said I.

'Nor have I. But the telegraph posts upon this line are sixty yards apart, and the calculation is a simple one.'

Commenting on this, Mr. Warrack maintains that to arrive at his result Holmes would have been obliged to work out in his head an arithmetical sum of overwhelming complexity, and that it would have been impossible with a pocket watch to time the passage of telegraph poles to the necessary tenth of a second. Mr. Warrack, if we may so express it, is making telegraph-poles out of fountain-pens. What happened, surely, was something like this: About half a minute before he addressed Watson, Holmes had looked at the second hand of his watch and had then counted fifteen telegraph poles (he had, of course, *seen* the quarter-mile posts, but had not *observed* them, since they were not to be the basis of his calculation). This would give him a distance of nine hundred yards, a fraction over half a mile. If a second glance at his watch had shown him that thirty seconds had passed, he would have known at once that the train was travelling at a good sixty miles an hour. Actually he noted that the train had taken approximately thirty-four seconds to cover the nine hundred yards; or, in other words, it was rather more than ten per cent. slower than a train travelling at sixty miles an hour, and Holmes accordingly deducted rather more than ten per cent. (i.e. $6\frac{1}{2}$) from sixty. The calculation, as he said, was a simple one; what made it simple for him was his knowledge, which of course Watson did not share, that the telegraph poles were sixty yards apart. Mr. Warrack's talk of 'sheer bluff' is manifestly irrelevant.

While we have felt it desirable, in the interests of Holmesian scholarship, to animadvert upon certain weaknesses in Mr. Warrack's line of argument, we must, nevertheless, conclude by repeating our welcome for his book. The production and proof-reading (save for an inaccuracy in the spelling of Mr. Desmond MacCarthy's name) are good, and the work is printed on paper of exceptional quality. We trust that Mr. Warrack will pursue his researches and reconsider some of his judgements.

(vi) *His kinship with Dr. Johnson*

Holmes's famous remark that he was lost without his Boswell has naturally led commentators to draw a comparison between the Holmes–Watson and the Johnson–Boswell association.[1]

[1] See, e.g. R. D. Altick, *Mr. Sherlock Holmes and Dr. Samuel Johnson* in *221B, Studies in Sherlock Holmes*, ed. Vincent Starrett (New York, 1940).

At first sight, the contrasts seem more striking than any resemblances. When Holmes and Watson were brought together by young Stamford, the two men were much of an age; when Boswell was introduced to Johnson by Tom Davies, Johnson was already the great man, while Boswell was a young celebrity-hunter, more than thirty years his junior. On the face of it, it would indeed seem absurd to liken the massive figure of the great moralist, the great clubman, the great talker (with no ear for music) to the lean, sunken-eyed recluse of Baker Street, whose principal recreation was his violin. Similarly, Boswell and Watson, considered by themselves, present few obvious resemblances. Watson, though not lacking in a spirit of adventure or in a taste for gambling, was fundamentally steady and respectable. Apart from one reference to a slight excess of Beaune at luncheon, his record of sobriety is a clean one and there is little reason to suppose that the details of his experience of women in three continents would furnish material comparable with that contained in Boswell's diaries. Nevertheless, if the two partnerships are broadly considered from the point of view of human relationship, a genuine likeness may well begin to emerge.

Holmes found in Watson as Johnson found in Boswell, the perfect foil. Each was immediately attracted to, and amused by, his new companion and in each case the first introduction was quickly followed by close association.

Of Boswell it was said that his good humour was

such that it was scarce a virtue. Holmes felt much the same about Watson; he would snub, and occasionally offend him, but friendliness was quickly restored.

Johnson found in Boswell 'a companion whose acuteness would help my enquiry and whose gaiety of conversation and civility of manners are sufficient to counteract the inconveniences of travel'. The extent to which Holmes relied upon Watson's acuteness as an aid to his investigations may be doubtful, but certainly he welcomed, and indeed was dependent upon, his civility as a travelling companion. Both Boswell and Watson were superbly good listeners.

At the very beginning of his *Journey to the Western Islands* Johnson remarks that neither Boswell nor the other gentleman who accompanied them at the time had ever troubled their heads about the Island of Inch Keith in the Firth of Forth, 'though, lying within their view, it had all their lives solicited their notice'. In other words, they had seen the island, but never observed it, just as Watson was unable to tell Holmes the number of steps leading up from the hall to the sitting-room of 221B.

In Johnson's and Holmes's general approach to life there is, indeed, a substantial element in common.

'Is not all life pathetic and futile?' exclaimed Holmes. 'We reach. We grasp. And what is left in our hands at the end? A shadow. Or worse than a shadow—misery.'

Here is the authentic voice of Rasselas—or of the Rambler, who declared that 'infelicity is involved in corporeal nature and interwoven with our being', and although both Johnson and Holmes were thus tinged with ultimate pessimism, they both recognized the importance of recording trivialities. 'I have found', said Holmes, 'that it is usually in unimportant matters that there is a field for observation.' So Johnson, amongst many other details, described with some care the imperfections of Scottish window-frames and became slightly apologetic: 'These diminutive observations seem to take away something from the dignity of writing . . . but it must be remembered that life consists not of a series of illustrious actions or elegant enjoyments; the greater part of our time passes in compliance with necessities, in the performance of daily duties. . . .'

Chemical experiment was, of course, a particular hobby of both men. 'Our chambers were always full of chemicals' Watson complained and we know both from Boswell and Mrs. Thrale how fond Johnson was not only of 'drawing essences and colouring liquors', but of making minute observations of varied kinds. When he accidentally shaved a finger-nail whilst sharpening a knife, he noted the exact position of the cut with a view to measuring the rate of growth of the nail; at another time, having cut 41 leaves from a vine and found them to weigh $5\frac{1}{2}$ ounces and 8 scruples, he laid them upon his bookcase to see what weight they would lose by drying. Here, surely, were activities and accuracies after Holmes's own heart.

But for Nature in the broader sense, neither had

a genuine love or interest. 'Appreciation of nature', writes Watson, 'found no place amongst his [Holmes's] many gifts'; and when Henry Thrale endeavoured to interest Johnson in the different dispositions of wood and water, hill and valley, Johnson replied: 'Never heed such nonsense, a blade of grass is always a blade of grass . . . let us if we *do* talk, talk about something; men and women are my subjects of enquiry.'

And how spontaneously each of them turned to London for recreation and inspiration.

'What do you say to a ramble through London?' said Holmes to Watson, and for three hours they strolled about together, 'watching the ever-changing kaleidoscope of life as it ebbs and flows through Fleet Street and the Strand.' Could Johnson, who gloried in the full tide of life at Charing Cross, have asked for anything better?

Finally: 'It is easy to guess the trade of an artizan by his knees, his fingers or his shoulders'. That is a quotation not from *A Study in Scarlet*, but from *The Rambler* (No. 173), and may serve to demonstrate that a comparison of Sherlock Holmes with Dr. Johnson is not a wholly fanciful exercise.

DR. WATSON

(i) *The chronological problem*

The recent publication [1928] of *The Complete Sherlock Holmes Short Stories*[1] and of *Essays in Satire*[2] offers a convenient opportunity for a brief commentary on the thesis presented in the latter volume by the learned Knocksius and entitled *Studies in the Literature of Sherlock Holmes.*

Knocksius's brilliant, if somewhat superficial, survey of the work of his predecessors in this field (Backnecke, Sauwosch, Piff-Pouff, Papier Mâché, and Ratzegger) undoubtedly has its merits as a *prolegomenon* to the study of *das Watsonischechronologieproblem*, but it is a matter for some surprise that this article, first written in 1911, should now be issued unrevised and without reference, even by way of a footnote, to the investigations of later scholarship. There is no mention, for instance, of the interesting, though not wholly convincing, theory put forward by Rendallus in 1917 to account for the solecisms inherent in *The Three Students.*[3]

---

[1] By Sir A. Conan Doyle (Murray).
[2] By R. A. Knox (Sheed and Ward).
[3] *The London Nights of Belsize* (1917), pp. 135 ff.

More serious, however, are the flagrant inaccuracies in the chronological tabulation of the *Adventures and Memoirs* as prepared by Knocksius (*Essays in Satire*, pp. 155, 156) and based on 'internal evidence, implicit or explicit'. Let us examine one or two examples of Knocksius's reckless handling of this evidence:

1. He writes:

To some period in the year '88 we must assign . . . the *Stockbroker's Clerk* . . . and the *Red-Headed League*.

There is little occasion for speculation in the matter of the date of either of these adventures, since in the second paragraph of *The Stockbroker's Clerk* Watson states explicitly that Holmes called on him *one morning in June, as he sat reading the British Medical Journal*. About the date of *The Red-Headed League*, Watson is even more explicit: the advertisement of a vacancy in the League appeared in *The Morning Chronicle* of 27 April 1890 and the notice of its dissolution on 9 October 1890. So much for Knocksius's 'some period in the year '88'.

2. Knocksius places *The Blue Carbuncle*, with a kind of ecclesiastical vagueness, 'somewhere in the octave of Christmas'. This is less serious, but in the interests of accurate scholarship, should not be passed without comment. Watson records in the first sentence that he called upon his friend *upon the second morning after Christmas*.

3. *The Copper Beeches*, according to Knocksius, is 'apparently before Watson's marriage'. We could

wish that Knocksius were less fond of the word 'apparently'. What is apparent to us is that in the course of this adventure Holmes refers to the Man with the Twisted Lip (June 1889—the year after Watson's marriage) as past history.

In justice to Knocksius it is only fair to say that the whole problem bristles with difficulties. Neither Keibosch nor Pauvremütte seems to us to have faced the central problem—the date of Watson's marriage. To review the whole evidence would be out of place here, but one or two of the major difficulties may be indicated in the interests of future research:

1. Watson became engaged in 1888 (*The Sign of Four*).

2. *The Crooked Man* is dated 'a few months after', and *The Naval Treaty* is assigned to 'the July which immediately succeeded' the marriage;

but

3. *A Scandal in Bohemia*, which is categorically dated 20 March 1888, occurs after marriage 'had drifted us [Watson and Holmes] away from each other'. The length, or width, of this drift is not specified, but in the course of it Holmes had been engaged on a successful mission on behalf of the Dutch royal house and had travelled to Odessa and back in connexion with the Trepoff murder. Watson had only heard of these things through the daily papers.

Knocksius places *A Scandal in Bohemia* between *The Crooked Man* and *The Naval Treaty*; the three adventures are to be dated, he says, 'apparently in that order'—on what grounds we have been unable to determine.

Knocksius's incursions into critical exegesis are not wholly fortunate. Following Backnecke in his attack upon the authenticity of *The Return* stories he writes:

> In the *Story of the Empty House* . . . the dummy . . . is draped in '*the old mouse-coloured dressing-gown*'! As if we had forgotten that it was in a *blue* dressing-gown that Holmes smoked an ounce of shag tobacco at a sitting, while he unravelled the dark complications of the *Man with the Twisted Lip*!

This is sound enough, so far as it goes; but it is to be feared that Knocksius has forgotten that it was in a *purple* dressing-gown that Holmes reclined upon the sofa when he tackled the problem of *The Blue Carbuncle*! Further, *The Blue Carbuncle* belongs to the *Adventures*, not to *The Return* series. Knocksius must at least abandon the shade of Holmes's dressing-gown as a test of canonicity.

We should read Knocksius's purely literary criticism with greater enjoyment if our confidence in his scholarship were not shaken by the fear that his texts are not wholly above suspicion. In his illustrations, for instance, of the highly important figure known to students as the *Sherlockismus* he quotes two passages. The first is the well-known dialogue from *Silver Blaze*:

> 'Let me call your attention to the curious incident of the dog in the night-time.'

'The dog did nothing at all in the night-time.'
'That was the curious incident,' said Sherlock Holmes.

It is possible that Knocksius has his own textual authority for what appears to us to be a wholly unwarrantable conflation. We do not claim to have made an entirely exhaustive study of each family of Watson texts, but in such editions as we have been able to consult, the passage runs:

'Is there any other point to which you would wish to draw my attention?'
'To the curious incident of the dog in the night-time.'
'The dog did nothing in the night-time.'
'That was the curious incident,' remarked Sherlock Holmes.

The interpolation of the superfluous *at all* and the substitution of the prosaic *said* for the more picturesque *remarked* do not argue well for a sense either of linguistic accuracy or of euphonious expression.

The second illustration is even more remarkable. No reference is given, but 'apparently' it is taken, without verification, from Ratzegger's notoriously unreliable *Collectanea*; and, unless we are mistaken, it is a quotation, or rather a reckless misquotation, from *The Devil's Foot*, a story which if Knocksius's hypothesis were accepted, would be excluded from the canon.

The whole problem of the composition of the latest collections (*His Last Bow* and *The Case-Book*) is outside the scope of Knocksius's paper, but one chronological point may be referred to here. In *The Veiled*

Lodger it is recorded that Sherlock Holmes was in active practice for twenty-three years. Now, Knocksius ascribes *A Study in Scarlet* to the year 1879. Twenty-three years from that date would bring us to the year 1902; yet *The Creeping Man* is explicitly dated 1903. Furthermore, we know that the battle in which Watson was wounded was fought in July 1880, so that his association with Holmes cannot possibly have begun before the later months of 1880.[1]

Finally, in the *Complete Short Stories* one observes a regrettable laxity in the simple matter of place-names. The adventure in which Holmes made his 'final exit' is described in the preface as 'The Adventure of Shoscombe Abbey', but in the text we find 'Shoscombe Old Place'. Trifles such as these may be of some interest to the amateur of textual collation, but it is to be hoped that serious students will rather devote their energies to the elucidation of the major problems of Watsonian chronology, the complexity of which we have sought but to adumbrate.

(ii) *His life*

'As in every phenomenon the Beginning remains always the most notable moment; so with regard to any great man, we rest not till, for our scientific profit or not, the whole circumstances of his first appearance in this Planet, and what manner of Public Entry he made, are with utmost completeness rendered manifest.'

[1] See pp. 68 ff.

So wrote Carlyle, an author from whose voluminous works quotations would readily fall from the lips of Dr. Watson himself. But to render manifest the whole circumstances of Watson's first appearance in this planet is a task before which Boswell himself might well have quailed. Certainly Boswell might have run half over London and fifty times up and down Baker Street with very little reward for his trouble. Where were the friends or relatives who could have given him the information about Watson's early life? 'Tadpole' Phelps might have given a few schoolboy anecdotes; young Stamford might have been traced to Harley Street or some provincial surgery, and have talked a little about Watson at Bart's; his brother had been a skeleton in the family cupboard; his first wife, as seems probable, died some five or six years after marriage; Holmes himself might have deduced much but, except in the famous instance of the fifty-guinea watch, seldom concerned himself with Watson's private affairs. The young Watson, in short, is an elusive figure. 'Data, data, give us data', as Holmes might have said.

Since he took his doctor's degree at the University of London in 1878, Watson's birth may with a fair measure of confidence be assigned to the year 1852.[1]

The place of his birth is wrapped in deeper mystery. At first sight the balance of evidence seems to point

[1] A distinguished surgeon, who proceeded to the London doctorate in the same year as Watson, was born in this year. It is of some interest to note that he was in 1916 Consulting Surgeon at Netley, the scene of Watson's own later training.

to his being a Londoner; much of his written work, at any rate, conveys the suggestion that he was most fully at home in the sheltering arms of the great metropolis: Baker Street, the Underground, hansom cabs, Turkish baths, November fogs—these, it would seem, are of the very stuff of Watson's life. On the other hand, when, broken in health and fortune, Watson stepped off the *Orontes* on to the Portsmouth jetty, he 'naturally gravitated to London, that great cesspool into which all the loungers and idlers of the Empire are irresistibly drained'. It is difficult to believe that Watson, in whose veins there flowed a current of honest sentiment, could thus have described his native city. On the whole, we incline to the view that he was born either in Hampshire or Berkshire; it was as he travelled to Winchester[1] ('the old English capital', as he nobly calls it) that he was moved by the beauty of the English countryside: 'the little white fleecy clouds . . . the rolling hills around Aldershot, the little red and grey roofs of the farm-steadings peeping out from amidst the light green of the new foliage'. 'Are they not fresh and beautiful?' he cried out to Holmes. . . . Again, Watson chafed at an August spent in London. It was not the heat that worried him (for an old Indian campaigner, as he said, a thermometer at 90° had no terrors); it was homesickness: he 'yearned for the glades of the New Forest or the shingle of Southsea. . . .'[2]

Concerning his parents Watson preserves a curious

[1] *The Copper Beeches.*   [2] *The Cardboard Box.*

silence. That his father (H. Watson) was, or had been, in comfortable circumstances may fairly be inferred from his possession of a fifty-guinea watch, and from his ability to leave his elder son with good prospects and to send his younger son to a school whence young gentlemen proceeded to Cambridge and the Foreign Office. Watson's reticence about his elder brother is hardly surprising: squandering the legacy bequeathed to him by his father he lived in poverty, 'with occasional short intervals of prosperity'. Possibly he was an artist who occasionally sold a picture; more probably he was a gambler. In any event, he died of drink round about the year 1886.[1]

Concerning Watson's boyhood two facts stand out clearly: he spent a portion of it in Australia, and he was sent to school in England. The reference to Australia is categorical. As he stood hand-in-hand with Miss Morstan in the grounds of Pondicherry Lodge, 'like two children', as he significantly says, the scenes of his own childhood came back to him: 'I have seen something of the sort on the side of a hill near Ballarat, where the prospectors had been at work'. In all probability, then, the period of Watson's Australian residence was before he reached the age of 13.[2]

[1] For a discussion of this date see *post*, p. 74. At the beginning of *The Sign of Four* Watson had 'quite recently' come into the possession of the watch.

[2] Watson and 'Tadpole' Phelps were 'little boys' together. On the other hand, it is just possible that Watson gained his knowledge of Australia later (see *post*, p. 73).

No reader of Watson's narrative can have failed to notice his curious treatment of his mother.[1] The explanation must surely lie in Mrs. Watson's early decease—probably very soon after her second son's birth. It is, perhaps, a little more fanciful—though not, surely, fantastic—to surmise that she was a devout woman with Tractarian leanings, and that before her death she breathed a last wish into her husband's ear that the child should be called John Henry, after the great Newman himself.

Unable to face life in the old home, Watson *père* set out to make a new life in Australia, taking his two young children with him. Whether he had good luck in the goldfields round Ballarat or in other spheres of speculative adventure, it is evident that he prospered. Of the influence of this Australian upbringing on the character of Dr. Watson we have abundant evidence: his sturdy common sense, his coolness, his adaptability to rough conditions on Dartmoor or elsewhere are marks of that tightening of moral and physical fibre which comes from the hard schooling of colonial life. Londoner as he afterwards became, Watson was always ready to doff the bowler hat, to slip his revolver into his coat pocket, and to face a mystery or a murder-gang with a courage which was as steady as it was unostentatious. But to return to Watson's boyhood: that he was sent to one of the public schools of England can hardly be doubted,

[1] The reader may reply: 'But Watson never mentions his mother.' 'That', as Holmes would say, 'is the curious treatment.'

since one of his intimate friends was Percy Phelps, the 'very brilliant boy' who, after a triumphant career at Cambridge, obtained a Foreign Office appointment. He was 'extremely well connected'. 'Even when we were all little boys together', writes Watson, 'we knew that his mother's brother was Lord Holdhurst, the great Conservative politician.' But Watson's sturdy colonialism was proof against the insidious poison of schoolboy snobbery, and took little account of Phelps's 'gaudy relationship'. The boy was designated by no more dignified name than 'Tadpole', and his fellows found it 'rather a piquant thing' to 'chevy him about the playground and hit him over the shins with a wicket'—a sentence which suggests that Watson's school, like many others, preserved certain peculiarities of vocabulary, keeping the old term 'play-ground' for 'playing-field' and using 'wicket' in the sense of 'stump'. That it was a 'rugger' school there can be little doubt. How else would Watson have played three-quarter for Blackheath in later years? Characteristically, Watson never alludes to his prowess on the football field, until he is reminded of it by 'big Bob Ferguson', who once 'threw him over the ropes into the crowd at the Old Deer Park'.[1] In class-work we may conclude that Watson was able, rather than brilliant; he was two forms below 'Tadpole' Phelps, though of the same age; his school number was thirty-one.[2]

Of Watson's student days we have but scanty

---

[1] *The Sussex Vampire.*　　　　[2] *The Retired Colourman.*

record. At St. Bartholomew's Hospital he found himself in an atmosphere that has always been steeped in the tradition of the literary physician,[1] and it is clear that Watson was not of those who are content with the broad highway of the ordinary textbook. The learned and highly specialized monograph of Percy Trevelyan upon certain obscure nervous lesions, though something of a burden to its publishers, had not escaped the eye of the careful Watson;[2] nor was he unfamiliar with the researches of French psychologists.[3] With such interests in the finer points of neurological technique, it may at first sight seem strange that Watson should have chosen the career of an army surgeon, but after what has already been said of Watson's colonial background, it is clear that in the full vigour of early manhood he could not face the humdrum life of the general practitioner. The appeal of a full, pulsing life of action, coupled with the camaraderie of a regimental mess, was irresistible. Accordingly, we find him proceeding to the army surgeon's course at Netley. Whether he played 'rugger' for the United Services is uncertain; his qualification as a 'Club' three-quarter was a high one, but it is probable that at this period his passion for horses was developed. His summer quarters were near Shoscombe in Berkshire, and the turf never lost its

---

[1] The names of Thomas Browne, William Osler, Norman Moore, and Geoffrey Keynes occur at once amongst many others. The late Poet Laureate could probably have contributed some interesting *Watsoniana.*

[2] *The Resident Patient.*   [3] *The Six Napoleons.*

attraction for him. Half of his wound pension, as he once confessed to Holmes, was spent on racing.[1]

But the scene was soon to be changed. At the end of his course Watson was duly posted to the Northumberland Fusiliers as Assistant Surgeon. With what zest may we picture him opening his account with Cox & Co. at Charing Cross,[2] and purchasing his tin trunk, pith helmet, and all the equipment necessary for Eastern service; with what quiet satisfaction must he have supervised the painting of the legend JOHN H. WATSON, M.D., upon his tin dispatch-box! But events were moving quickly; before Watson could join his regiment, the Second Afghan War had broken out.

It was in the spring of 1880 that Watson embarked, in company with other officers, for service in our Indian dominion. At Bombay he received intelligence that his corps 'had advanced through the passes and was already deep in the enemy's country'. At Kandahar, which had been occupied by the British in July,[3] Watson joined his regiment, but it was not with his own regiment that he was destined to go into action: 'The Fifth marched back to Peshawar, and from there to Lawrencepore; and . . . in September they received orders for home. . . . So they turned their backs on the tragedy of Maiwand.'[4] To Watson, however, the battle of Maiwand, fought on 27 July 1880, was to

[1] *Shoscombe Old Place.*   [2] *Thor Bridge.*
[3] Walker, *History of the Northumberland Fusiliers*, p. 414.
[4] Ibid.

67

become only too vivid a memory. He was removed from his own brigade and attached to the Berkshires (the 66th Foot), the story of whose heroic resistance at Maiwand has passed into military history.[1] Early in the course of the engagement, but not before he had, without loss of nerve, seen his comrades hacked to pieces,[2] Watson had been struck on the left shoulder by a Jezail bullet. The bone was shattered and the bullet grazed the subclavian artery; but, thanks to his orderly, Murray, to whose courage and devotion Watson pays a marked tribute, he was saved from falling into the hands of 'the murderous Ghazis', and after a pack-horse journey which must have aggravated the pain of the wounded limb, reached the British lines in safety. Of Watson's comrades-in-arms we know little; but seven years later we find his referring to his 'old friend Colonel Hayter' as having come under his professional care in Afghanistan.[3] Hayter is described as 'a fine old soldier who had seen much of the world', and it would seem fairly safe to identify him with the Major Charles Hayter who was director of Kabul Transport in the Second Afghan War.[4]

The story of Watson's experiences in the base hospital at Peshawar, of his gradual convalescence, of his severe attack of enteric fever ('that curse', in his own graphic phrasing, 'of our Indian possessions'), of his final discharge, and of his return to England

[1] See Hanna, *The Second Afghan War*, iii. 416.
[2] *A Study in Scarlet.*   [3] *The Reigate Squires.*
[4] Hanna, op. cit., pp. 470, 525.

either late in 1880 or early in 1881, may be read in the pages of his own narrative.[1]

With no kith or kin in England, with a broken constitution and a pension of 11s. 6d. a day, a man of weaker fibre than John H. Watson might well have sunk into dejection or worse. But Watson quickly realized the dangers of his comfortless and meaningless existence: even the modest hotel in the Strand he found to be beyond his means. Standing one day in the Criterion bar, 'as thin as a lath and as brown as a nut', he was tapped on the shoulder by young Stamford, who had been a dresser under him at Bart's. Overjoyed to see a friendly face, Watson immediately carried him off to lunch at the Holborn, where he explained his most pressing need—cheap lodgings. Young Stamford looked 'rather strangely' over his wine-glass. Had he some kind of intuition that he was to be one of the great liaison-officers of literary history, that he was shortly to bring about a meeting comparable in its far-reaching influences with that other meeting arranged by Tom Davies in Russell Street, Covent Garden, more than a hundred years before?

Taking Watson with him to the chemical laboratory at St. Bartholomew's, young Stamford fulfilled his mission:

'Dr. Watson, Mr. Sherlock Holmes. . . .'

'How are you? . . . You have been in Afghanistan, I perceive.'

'How on earth did you know that? . . .'

[1] *A Study in Scarlet.*

Such was the initiatory dialogue. Holmes and Watson quickly agreed to share rooms,[1] and the load of depression was lifted from Watson's mind. Life had a new interest for him; the element of mystery about his prospective fellow-lodger struck him as 'very piquant'; as he aptly quoted to young Stamford: 'the proper study of mankind is man. . . .'

The walls of No. 221B Baker Street[2] bear no commemorative tablet. It is doubtful indeed whether the house has survived the latter-day onslaught of steel and concrete. Yet Baker Street remains for ever permeated with the Watsonian aura. The dim figures of the Baker Street Irregulars scuttle through the November gloom, the ghostly hansom drives away, bearing Holmes and Watson on an errand of mystery.

For some time Holmes himself remained a mystery to his companion. But on 4 March 1881 he revealed himself as a consulting detective ('probably the only one in the world'), and on the same day there came Inspector Gregson's letter relating to the Lauriston Gardens Mystery. After much hesitation Holmes decided to take up the case. 'Get your hat', he called to Watson; and though Watson accompanied his friend to the Brixton Road with little enthusiasm, Holmes's brusque summons was in fact

---

[1] Holmes had rooms in Montague Street when he first came to London (*The Musgrave Ritual*).

[2] Dr. Gray C. Briggs, of St. Louis, deduced that the house in which Holmes and Watson lived was No. 111 Baker Street (see F. D. Steele, *Sherlock Holmes*). See also J. E. Holroyd, *221B Baker Street?* in the *Cornhill*, No. 987, 1951.

a trumpet-call to a new life for Watson. In the course
of the adventure which is known to history as *A Study
in Scarlet*, Watson's alertness as a medical man is
immediately evident. His deduction of the solubility
in water of the famous pill was quick and accurate;
nor did he fail to diagnose an aortic aneurism in
Jefferson Hope. 'The walls of his chest', he recorded
in his graphic way, 'seemed to thrill and quiver as a
frail building would do inside when some powerful
engine was at work. In the silence of the room I could
hear a dull humming and buzzing noise which proceeded from the same source.' At this stage the friendship between Watson and Holmes was only in the
making: Holmes still addressed his companion as
'Doctor'. But it was in his first adventure that Watson found his true *métier*. 'I have all the facts in my
journal and the public shall know them.'

Between 1881 and 1883 (the year of *The Speckled
Band*) we have little record of Watson's doings.
Possibly he divided his time quietly between Baker
Street and his club. More probably he spent a portion
of this period abroad. His health and spirits were
improving; he had no family ties in England; Holmes
was at times a trying companion. Now in later years
Watson refers to 'an experience of women which
extends over many nations and three separate continents'.[1] The three continents are clearly Europe,
India, and Australia. In Australia he had been but a
boy; in India he can have seen few women except the

[1] *The Sign of Four.*

71

staff-nurses at Peshawar. It is conceivable, though not likely, that he revisited Australia at this time. It is much more probable that Watson spent some time on the Continent and that, in particular, he visited such resorts as contained the additional attraction of a casino. Gambling was the ruling passion of the Watson family. Watson *père* had gambled on his luck as an Australian prospector—and won; his elder son gambled on life—and lost; the younger son (a keen racing man[1] and a dabbler in stocks and shares[2]) no doubt won, and lost, at *rouge et noir*.

By the time of *The Speckled Band* it is noteworthy that the intimacy between Watson and Holmes has very considerably developed. Watson is no longer 'Doctor' but 'My dear Watson'; Holmes's clients are bidden to speak freely in front of his 'intimate friend and associate'; if there is danger afoot, Watson has but one thought: Can he be of help? 'Your presence', Holmes told him in the case of the Speckled Band, 'might be invaluable.' 'Then', comes the quick reply, 'I shall certainly come.' It is the old campaigner who speaks.

The years 1884 and 1885 are again barren of detailed Watsonian record; and here again it is possible that Watson spent part of his time on the Continent. But with the year 1886 we approach one of the major biographical problems of Watson's career— the date of his first marriage.

[1] See *ante*, pp. 67, 68.
[2] *The Dancing Men.*

For a proper consideration of the problem it is necessary, first, to clear one's mind of sentiment. We may remember Holmes's own criticism of Watson's first narrative: 'Detection is, or ought to be, an exact science, and should be treated in the same cold and unemotional manner. You have attempted to tinge it with romanticism. . . .'

The biographer, when he reaches the story of Watson's courtship, must necessarily endeavour to do justice to its idyllic quality, but, primarily, he is concerned with a problem. Let us review our data:

1. In *The Sign of Four*, Miss Morstan, according to Watson's narrative, used the phrase: 'About six years ago—to be exact, upon the 4th May, 1882. . . .' This would appear to date the adventure between April and June 1888.

2. *A Scandal in Bohemia* is specifically dated 20 March 1888, and evidently occurred a considerable time after Watson's marriage. Watson had drifted away from Baker Street, and Holmes had been far afield—in Holland and Odessa.

3. At the time of *The Reigate Squires*, April 1887, Holmes and Watson were still together in Baker Street.

4. The adventure of *The Five Orange Pips* is dated September 1887, and occurred after Watson's marriage (his wife was visiting her aunt and he had taken the opportunity to occupy his old quarters at Baker Street).

A brief summary of this kind does not, of course, pretend to include all the available data, but is at least sufficient to indicate certain contradictions which Holmes himself would have found difficult to reconcile.

Suppose, for instance, that we accept the traditional date for Watson's engagement to Miss Morstan—the year 1888. In that case the marriage cannot have taken place until the late summer or autumn of that year. What, then, becomes of the extremely precise dating of *A Scandal in Bohemia* and *The Five Orange Pips*?

One thing is clear: Watson, careful chronicler as he is, cannot have been consistently accurate in his dates. The traditional assignment of *The Sign of Four* to the year 1888 rests upon Watson's report of Miss Morstan's conversation; the dates of *The Reigate Squires* and of *The Five Orange Pips* are first-hand statements of Watson himself.

Now Watson, when he wrote the journal of *The Sign of Four*, cannot be said to have been writing in his normal, business-like condition. From the moment that Miss Morstan entered the sitting-room of No. 221B Baker Street, he was carried away by what he picturesquely calls 'mere will-o'-the wisps of the imagination'. He tried to read Winwood Reade's *Martyrdom of Man*, but in vain; his mind ran upon Miss Morstan—'her smiles, the deep, rich tones of her voice, the strange mystery which overhung her life'. Further, the Beaune he had taken for lunch had, on his own confession, affected him, and he had been brought to a pitch of exasperation by Holmes's extreme deliberation of manner. On the whole, then, was this a state of mind calculated to produce chronological accuracy?

On the other hand, there are no such reasons to make us doubt the accuracy of *The Reigate Squires* and *The Five Orange Pips*; and if we accept the dates of these, the marriage must be fixed between April and September 1887. Now, assuming that Miss Morstan shared the common prejudice against the unlucky month, it is not likely that the ceremony took place in May. June, on the other hand, seems extremely probable, since *The Naval Treaty* (July 1887) is described as 'immediately succeeding the marriage'.

Accordingly, we are driven to conclude that *The Sign of Four* belongs to the year 1886, in the autumn of which Watson became engaged. In the early part of 1887 Watson would be busy buying a practice, furnishing a house, and dealing with a hundred other details. This would explain why, of the very large number of cases with which Holmes had to deal in this year, Watson has preserved full accounts of only a few. He had made rough notes, but had no time to elaborate them. 'All these',[1] he writes in a significant phrase, 'I may sketch out at some future date.' Again, if June 1887 be accepted as the date of the marriage, the opening of *A Scandal in Bohemia* becomes for the first time intelligible. Between June 1887 and March

[1] The Paradol Chamber, the Amateur Mendicant Society, &c. (see *The Five Orange Pips*).

1888 there was plenty of time for Watson to put on seven pounds in weight as the result of married happiness and for Holmes to attend to separate summonses from Odessa and The Hague.

To claim definite certainty for such a solution would be extravagant; but as a working hypothesis it has claims which cannot be lightly dismissed.

Whatever may have been the exact date of Watson's marriage with Miss Morstan,[1] it would seem clear that in the early years, at least, of his married life Watson achieved the happiness which he desired and deserved. Such glimpses as he gives us of his hearth and home suggest a picture of domestic Bohemianism which was in complete harmony with Watson's temperament. So long as he had believed that Miss Morstan might be a rich heiress, his delicate sense of honour had prevented him from declaring his passion. But when it was finally known that the Agra treasure was lost and that the 'golden barrier' (to use Watson's own picturesque phrase) was removed, Watson could rejoice in the prospect of sharing the simple home of a middle-aged practi-

---

[1] Mr. R. I. Gunn, to whose work upon the various problems of Watsonian chronology I am deeply indebted, places Watson's marriage in the October, not in the June, of 1887. This assignment is based on various statements in *The Noble Bachelor*, which constitutes a strong argument in Mr. Gunn's favour. On the other hand, the dating (September 1887) of *The Five Orange Pips* is precise and Watson's reference to his wife's visit to her aunt is clear and categorical. It is in any case satisfactory to note the growing agreement amongst scholars as to the *year* of Watson's marriage with Miss Morstan. (See, for instance, Desmond MacCarthy's paper in *The Listener* for 11 December 1929.)

tioner with one whom even Holmes described as one of the most charming young ladies he had ever met. Holmes, indeed, went further: he regarded the marriage of Miss Morstan as a loss to the detective profession. 'She had a decided genius that way', he admitted to Watson—high praise, indeed, from Holmes, exceeded only by his admiration for Irene Adler, who 'eclipsed and predominated' the whole of her sex in the detective's eyes.

But to return to Watson's marriage. Of the ceremony itself we have no specific record. We may, however, assume that it was not marred by any vulgar ostentation. If Miss Morstan on her first visit to Baker Street gave the impression of a small and dainty blonde, 'well gloved and dressed in the most perfect taste', we may safely conjecture that the 'plainness and simplicity' which Watson then noted in her costume were also the predominant characteristics of her bridal appearance. Whether Holmes was induced to be best man is at least doubtful, since Watson would hardly be likely to omit a record of so personal a tribute; with the exception of one aunt, neither Watson nor his bride had relatives living; consequently it seems most probable that the ceremony took place very quietly at St. Mark's or St. Hilda's, Camberwell,[1] with Miss Morstan's aunt and Mrs. Forrester present to give their blessing.

[1] It is possible, of course, that the marriage took place at a register office. But, on the whole, Watson and his bride are likely to have preferred a religious service. Each of them spontaneously thanked God at the time of their betrothal.

The honeymoon (spent probably in Hampshire, a county for which Watson had a strong sentimental attachment[1]) was no doubt a short one, as Watson had much to do in refashioning his career. Turning instinctively to a neighbourhood not far removed from Baker Street, he found what he wanted in the Paddington district. There a certain Mr. Farquhar had built up an excellent general practice which had, at its best, brought in the substantial income of £1,200 a year. But Mr. Farquhar had been overtaken not only by old age but by a species of St. Vitus's dance. Now the public, as Watson shrewdly observes, 'looks askance at the curative powers of the man whose own case is beyond the reach of his drugs' and, in consequence, the practice had declined to about one-quarter of its range and value. Here was Watson's opportunity. Confident in his own energy and ability, he bought the practice, with a determination to restore it to its previously flourishing condition. Three months of hard work followed. Watson was too busy even to visit 221B Baker Street, and Holmes 'seldom went anywhere except on professional business'.[2] Further, such leisure as he had Watson instinctively devoted to his wife and to his home. Completely happy, and half a stone heavier, he found his attention wholly absorbed by 'the home-centred interests which rise up round the man who first finds himself master of his own establishment'.[3] Of course, the Watsons were

---

[1] *Ante*, p. 63.   [2] *The Stockbroker's Clerk.*
[3] *A Scandal in Bohemia.*

not free from the normal troubles of modern domesticity. In their early married days they were obliged, no doubt, to be content with one servant, Mary Jane; she, as Watson records, proved to be incorrigible and was dismissed. Later it was found possible to increase the staff and Watson would write naturally of 'the servants'.[1]

Harmonious as it was, there was nothing irritatingly uxorious about the Watson *ménage*. In the September following the marriage, Mrs. Watson went for a few days to stay with her aunt and Watson himself took up his old quarters in Baker Street. Very naturally he slipped into his old place by the fireside, burying himself in one of Clark Russell's 'fine sea stories', while Holmes on the other side of the fireplace cross-indexed his criminal records.[2]

But this visit, though entirely amicable, seems to have left little permanent mark upon Watson's memory. It had not really brought Holmes within the orbit of Watson's matrimonial happiness. Hastening back, no doubt, to the devoted partner of his new life and to his rapidly growing practice, Watson plunged into his work, without any feeling of having truly re-entered into the old atmosphere of Baker Street. With a certain fineness of taste, he hesitated to drag Holmes into a social circle towards which the detective's 'whole Bohemian soul' might be antipathetic, and it was not until 20 March 1888 that he was moved with a keen desire to revisit his old friend. Returning from

[1] *The Crooked Man.*   [2] *The Five Orange Pips.*

a visit to a patient he found himself opposite 'the well-remembered door' in Baker Street and in a few minutes was back in the old room. Watson could hardly have chosen a better moment for his re-entry upon the Baker Street stage, since Holmes had just received the note which was to herald the visit of Wilhelm Gottsreich Sigismond von Ormstein, Grand Duke of Cassel-Falstein and hereditary King of Bohemia. On the following afternoon Watson was back at three o'clock, and for the rest of the day he was engaged in playing an important role in the comedy of the King's photograph; he slept at Baker Street in order to be ready for the denouement of the following morning.

This intermittent resumption of partnership with Holmes was characteristic of Watson's early married life, and at first sight might seem to indicate an element of restlessness in Watson's domestic milieu. But a closer study of the records shows that Mrs. Watson maintained a continuous sympathy with that association of Watson with the great detective which had been the means of bringing her to the man she loved. Holmes, for his part, maintained his respect for Mrs. Watson, and Mrs. Watson never failed to encourage her husband to collaborate with his old friend in any investigation in which he could be of use. Thus Holmes would descend upon Watson near midnight, ask for a bed, and carry off his friend by the eleven o'clock train from Waterloo the next morning;[1]

---

[1] *The Crooked Man.*

if an old friend of Watson was in trouble, his wife would acquiesce at once in his rushing off to Holmes;[1] when Watson received a telegram from Holmes urging him to come to the west of England for two days in connexion with the Boscombe Valley case, it was his wife who pressed him to go—the change, she said, would do him good.

Side by side with this ready sympathy of Mrs. Watson with her husband's bachelor associations we must recognize the atmosphere of domestic compatibility which characterized Watson's home life. It has been truly said that there are two tests of a happy marriage: first, a harmonious breakfast, and second, an acceptance of quiet evenings. That Watson and his wife breakfasted together we have categorical evidence;[2] and more than once we obtain a glimpse of evening contentment. Watson, after a busy day, would read a novel or his *British Medical Journal*; his wife would have her needlework; about ten-thirty the servants would be heard locking the doors and windows; half an hour later Mrs. Watson would retire; and about eleven forty-five Watson would knock out the ashes of his last pipe.[3] It is a picture which may be scoffed at as dull, prosaic, bourgeois; but it is nevertheless significant. After a varied experience of femininity, Watson was contentedly anchored in this haven of domesticity. Holmes, however, never ceased to regard Watson as a 'ladies'

[1] *The Naval Treaty.*
[2] *The Boscombe Valley Mystery.*　　　　[3] *The Crooked Man.*

man'. 'Now, Watson,' he would say, 'the fair sex is your department'; and when the Baker Street apartment was honoured by a visit from 'the most lovely woman in London',[1] it was Watson who recorded, in graphic phrasing, how 'the dwindling *frou-frou* of skirts had ended in the slam of the door'.

Of Watson's medical practice it is regrettable that we have no connected account. There can be little doubt that, having taken over a practice which had very much declined, he succeeded by assiduous devotion to his patients in building up a very satisfactory connexion. Thus in April 1888 he was absorbed in a case of great gravity, spending whole days at the bedside of the sufferer;[2] in the June of the same year he notes that he had been kept 'very close at work'[3] and Holmes deduced on one of his sudden visits that Watson was busy enough to justify the hansom. Again, a year later, Watson notes that late in the evening he was 'newly come back from a weary day'.[4] By this time his practice had steadily increased and his proximity to Paddington had brought him some patients from among the Great Western Railway officials.[5] At the time of the Adventure of the Blue Carbuncle (probably the Christmas of 1889) Watson was evidently still busy. He did not call upon Holmes to wish him the compliments of the season until the 27th of December, and a case delayed him on that day

---

[1] *The Second Stain.*   [2] *A Case of Identity.*
[3] *The Stockbroker's Clerk.*   [4] *The Man with the Twisted Lip.*
[5] *The Engineer's Thumb.*

until nearly half-past six. By the autumn of the year 1890, however, a complete change had come over Watson's professional life: 'I have nothing to do to-day', he would tell Holmes. 'My practice is never very absorbing';[1] and when Holmes invited him six months later to accompany him to the Continent at a day's notice, there was no hesitation: 'The practice is quiet', said Watson, 'and I have an accommodating neigh-bour.[2] I should be glad to come.' Watson's readiness to leave home was partly due, no doubt, to the fact that his wife was also away, and it is difficult to resist the conclusion that it was about this time that Mrs. Watson's health began to fail. Watson's resumption of professional work was so closely bound up with his devotion to his wife and his home-life, that some major cause must be sought for the relatively sudden decline of his interest in his practice. Now Mrs. Watson died some time between the summer of 1891 and the spring of 1894, the period during which Watson believed his friend to be lying, a mangled corpse, at the foot of the Reichenbach. Watson's own reference to his loss is characteristically slight. Holmes, on his return, referred sympathetically to his old colleague's bereavement and reminded him that work was the best antidote to sorrow. Actually Watson had already acted upon this advice. The falling-off of his professional activity which we have already noted began quite evidently in 1891 and it seems likely that the

---

[1] *The Red-Headed League.*
[2] More probably Jackson than Anstruther.

phrase 'my wife was away at the time' has a sad and sinister significance. In all probability Mrs. Watson had left for a period of treatment at a rest-home or sanatorium which unhappily proved to be of no avail. The long period of hoping against hope no doubt militated against her husband's vigorous prosecution of his professional work, but when the end came (probably in 1893) Watson roused himself from his grief as he had previously roused himself from the apathy of a half-pay officer invalided home from India. By the spring of 1894 his day was filled by his professional round.[1] That he should wish to sever himself from the sadness of his Paddington associations was natural. Accordingly we find him established in Kensington, in a small bachelor suite, with one maid to look after him. Undoubtedly the strain of the three years had told upon him. It is true that the manner of Holmes's return was sufficiently melodramatic to accelerate the most sluggish pulse, but it is hardly enough to account for an old campaigner like Watson falling into a dead faint. Clearly, his constitution had not fully recovered from the ravages of recent grief and worry. In the long run, nothing could have contributed so valuably to the restoration of Watson's health and enthusiasm as the reappearance of Sherlock Holmes. 'It was indeed like old times', he writes, 'when I found myself seated beside him in a hansom, my revolver in my pocket and the thrill of adventure in my heart.' The next step was inevitable. At the

[1] 'All day as I drove upon my round' (*The Empty House*).

end of a few months Watson had sold his practice in Kensington to a young doctor named Verner, and received a surprisingly high price for it. It was not until some years afterwards that Watson discovered that Verner was a distant relation of Holmes who had, in fact, found the money. It is rare, indeed, to come upon a reference to Holmes's family,[1] but what is still more interesting about this episode is the evidence which it provides of Holmes's eagerness to have Watson back in Baker Street.

For the next few years Watson, as chronicler, was destined to be extremely busy: the year of Holmes's return (1894) produced 'three massive manuscript volumes' of notes on cases and in 1895 Holmes was 'never in better form'. At the same time Watson retained some of his old professional interests. On a November night, while Holmes tackled a palimpsest, he would bury himself in a recent treatise upon surgery.[2] In many respects Watson shared Holmes's tastes: in particular they both derived great pleasure from the opera and from the Turkish bath. On the other hand, Watson remained a good clubman, whilst Holmes preferred to remain at home with his microscope and card-indexes.[3] It is evident, however, that Holmes kept the watchful eye of an elder brother upon Watson's gambling propensities. Watson played

[1] Possibly the name Verner is a corruption of Vernet, the French family to which Holmes's grandmother belonged.
[2] *The Golden Pince-Nez.*
[3] It is on record, however, that he found the atmosphere of the Diogenes Club a soothing one (*The Greek Interpreter*).

billiards with one man only and his cheque-book was safely locked in Holmes's drawer.[1] Taken as a whole, the years 1894 to 1901 formed a happy period in Watson's life. Holmes was throughout that time a very busy man; every public case of importance and hundreds of private cases were brought to him for solution and Watson, himself personally engaged in many of them, preserved 'very full notes' of the whole series. The adventures entailed much interesting travel: Watson might find himself at short notice in the National Hotel at Lausanne[2] or in furnished lodgings in an ancient university town; Holmes's researches in Early English charters led them to Oxford and the painful scandal of the Fortescue scholarship; a sudden visit from Cyril Overton, of Trinity ('sixteen stone of solid bone and muscle' and 'skipper of the Rugger team of Cambridge 'Varsity') led them to an inn (next to a bicycle shop) in Cambridge and to the sad end (at Trumpington) of the landlady's daughter who was 'as good as she was beautiful and as intelligent as she was good'.[3] Holmes, for his part, rejoiced to have Watson with him when he was engaged on a case. 'A confederate', he wrote, 'who foresees your conclusions and course of action is always dangerous, but one to whom each development comes as a perpetual surprise, and to whom the future is always a closed book, is indeed an ideal helpmate.'

More and more, as time went on, Holmes dis-

---

[1] *The Dancing Men.*   [2] *Lady Frances Carfax.*
[3] *The Missing Three-Quarter.*

played an affection for Watson which was very different from the casual camaraderie of their earlier association. At the crisis of the adventure of the Bruce-Partington Plans, Holmes acknowledged Watson's loyalty with a warm grip of the hand and Watson saw 'something in his eyes which was nearer to tenderness than I had ever seen'; in the adventure of the Devil's Foot it was Watson's prompt courage that saved Holmes from the 'freezing horror' of his own experiment. It was in an unsteady voice that Holmes expressed his thanks. Watson had never seen so much of Holmes's heart before. . . .

In the autumn of 1902 Holmes reached what Watson describes as, in some ways, the supreme moment of his career. This was in the matter of *The Illustrious Client* whose anonymity has been preserved to this day. Watson, it will be remembered, played a vital part in the outwitting of the notorious Baron Adelbert Gruner and was personally complimented by Holmes, who, having been enabled to confront Miss de Merville with categorical evidence of the Baron's sinister record, was at length able to secure the breaking-off of the engagement. Now it is significant that the next adventure to be recorded[1] is from the pen, not of Watson, but of Holmes himself. Why? Partly because Watson, with characteristic pertinacity, had worried him to try the job of writing himself and partly because, in Holmes's own words, 'the good Watson had at that time [i.e. January 1903] deserted

[1] *The Blanched Soldier.*

me for a wife, the only selfish action which I can recall in our association'. Here is categorical evidence
of prime importance, and the dating is precise.[1]

Who was the second Mrs. Watson? Once more
Watson's reticence is baffling. Beyond the indication
that after this date he was no longer living at Baker
Street, Watson tells us nothing of his second adventure in matrimony, and the biographer is thrown back
upon conjecture. Two main alternatives offer themselves for speculation: either Watson had been for
some time contemplating a second marriage, or it
was a sudden decision hastened by a dramatic crisis
in his life. In favour of the first theory it may be
claimed that in September 1902 Watson had already
moved to rooms in Queen Anne Street,[2] which might
well suggest that he already had changes in view; on
the other hand he was still enjoying the 'pleasant
lassitude' of the drying-room of a Turkish bath in
Holmes's company. The second theory rests upon a
more interesting conjecture: Watson's second marriage took place at the end of 1902 or at the beginning
of 1903, a few months after the affair of the Illustrious
Client. Now this adventure must have made a more
than ordinary impression upon Watson's mind.
Instinctively chivalrous, he was a man to whom a

---

[1] Holmes's reference to Watson's marriage at this date has misled some commentators (e.g. Mr. A. A. Milne in *By Way of Introduction*, p. 9). The suggestion that Watson married a second time
was first made to me by my friend Mr. Charles Carrington, and a
careful study of the chronology has provided ample confirmation.

[2] *The Illustrious Client.*

woman in trouble made a specially vivid appeal.[1] Violet de Merville, moreover, was 'beautiful, accomplished, a wonder-woman in every way'. After the terrible exposure of the true character of her *fiancé*, what more natural than that Watson should, after a fitting interval, make inquiries as to her recovery of health and spirits? Furthermore, had not Watson acquired a peculiar technique, so to speak, in his previous courtship of Miss Morstan? It may be objected that Miss de Merville moved in exalted circles, and that a retired practitioner would not have the *droit d'entrée* to her society. But here a significant fact must be considered. Miss de Merville's father was a soldier, and a soldier who had won distinction in Afghanistan—'de Merville of Khyber fame'. With such a father-in-law Watson would at once be on common ground. In any event, with Watson's second marriage his close and continuous association with Holmes came to an end. Their relations continued to be of the friendliest character and Holmes did not scruple to send for his old colleague 'when it was a case of active work and a comrade was needed' upon whose nerve he could place some reliance.[2]

Of Watson's own way of life after his second marriage we have unfortunately little or no evidence.

---

[1] It is noteworthy that, in making a selection from a very large number of Holmes's cases, Watson showed a marked preference for those in which a distressed gentlewoman was involved. Cf., especially, *A Case of Identity, The Speckled Band, The Copper Beeches, The Solitary Cyclist, Charles Augustus Milverton, The Second Stain, The Veiled Lodger.*   [2] *The Creeping Man.*

Whether his removal to Queen Anne Street was the result of a determination to engage in medical practice for a third time is not wholly clear. Much depends upon the canonicity of *The Mazarin Stone*. If the record of this adventure be accepted as a genuine compilation from Watson's notes, it is clear that the case belongs to a period some time after *The Empty House* and also after Watson's second removal from Baker Street; it is equally clear that Watson was a busy practitioner at the time.[1] Possibly Watson was now turning his attention to surgery,[2] and certainly his practice in September 1903 was 'not inconsiderable'.[3]

Of Holmes's later career, on the other hand, one fact is tolerably clear: by 1907 he had definitely retired from professional work. Though Watson seldom came into contact with him, the old friendship persisted and occasionally Watson would spend a week-end at Holmes's Sussex cottage. But here again there is no hint of how or where Watson was living.

It is not until 2 August 1914 that we get another —and final—glimpse of Watson. Here we are dependent upon an editorial hand, though it is difficult not to believe that the opening paragraph of *His Last Bow* is not taken verbatim from Watson's notes:

It was nine o'clock at night upon the 2nd August—the most terrible August in the history of the world. One might have thought already that God's curse hung heavy over a

---

[1] Assuming the record to be genuine, the editor may well have been the second Mrs. Watson, who would naturally take a proud interest in the part played by her husband in this adventure.

[2] *Ante*, p. 86.   [3] *The Creeping Man*.

degenerate world, for there was an awesome hush and a feeling of vague expectancy in the sultry and stagnant air.

Holmes, as we should expect, had not been lost sight of by His Majesty's Government in the years preceding the war. Not only Sir Edward Grey, but the Prime Minister himself, had waited upon him in his humble cottage in Sussex, and for two years Holmes had laboured to outwit the notorious Von Bork. That the great detective should summon his old comrade to play a part in the final act of the drama of espionage is one of the most striking tributes to the strength of the old friendship. It is clear that for some years before 1914 there had been no meeting. 'How have the years used you?' was Holmes's question. Watson on his part was, as ever, prompt and enthusiastic in answering the telegraphic summons to meet Holmes at Harwich, and there can be no doubt that he had prospered in his second matrimonial venture. He was by this time the owner of a motor-car and to Holmes he seemed 'the same blithe boy as ever'—a remarkable tribute to an old campaigner of sixty-two. What further part Watson took in the war remains unknown. It is doubtful whether he was permitted, at such an age, to proceed on foreign service, but we may be confident that in some capacity, possibly on the staff of a military hospital, he was at the post of duty. . . .

In August 1763 Johnson walked down to the beach at Harwich with his friend James Boswell; there the friends 'embraced and parted with tenderness'. In August 1914 Sherlock Holmes and Dr. Watson looked out at the moonlit sea at Harwich and talked 'in intimate converse':

'There's an east wind coming, Watson.'

'I think not, Holmes. It is very warm.'

'Good old Watson! You are the one fixed point in a changing age.'

THE BAKER STREET SCENE

(i) 221ᴮ *In retrospect*[1]

Number 221ʙ Baker Street! How richly the historical and emotional content of that simple address has developed in recent years! Where was, where is, 221ʙ? I am not concerned to argue about the precise identification of the site. Much topographical and cartographical study has been devoted to the subject;[2] but for my present purpose I am simply contemplating the rooms in Abbey House, just opposite the side entrance to Baker Street station, in which there is displayed a remarkable assembly of books, manuscripts, photographs, scientific specimens, and other items relating to the life and adventures of Sherlock Holmes. Let me add at once, however, that in one section of the exhibition the topographical enthusiast will find a large number of maps, plans, and photographs relating to 221ʙ which will keep him busy, and happy, for a considerable time.

As for the exhibition in general, there are one or two items that are almost terrifying to the unscientific and unsuspecting visitor. Take 'The Lion's Mane', for instance. It will be remembered that this story constitutes one of the few records of how Holmes spent his days after he had given himself up entirely

[1] A survey of the Sherlock Holmes Exhibition, 1951.
[2] See p. 71, n.

to the soothing life of Nature in his little Sussex home. It will be remembered, too, how, taking a walk along the cliff one morning in July 1907, he suddenly came face to face with tragedy in the mysterious death of Fitzroy McPherson while bathing from the beach; how the local police were baffled and how in a flash Holmes recalled an article by the Rev. J. G. Wood on *Cyanea Capillata*, the Lion's Mane, the 'curious waving, vibrating, hairy creature with streaks of silver among its yellow tresses'. Well, in the exhibition there is not only a copy of Wood's book (entitled *Out of Doors*) but a specimen of *Cyanea Capillata*. Unfortunately the zoologists seem a little doubtful about the killing capacity of this revolting jelly-fish and it is conjectured that McPherson's death may, in fact, have been caused by *Physalia*, an aggregate of jelly-fish organisms and a far more formidable object to a bather. I am in no way competent to discuss such matters—scientific investigators must examine the specimens, both of which are sufficiently repulsive, for themselves.

A similar problem appears to arise over a much more famous adventure—that of the Speckled Band. As we all know, the 'peculiar yellow band, with brownish speckles' which 'seemed to be bound tightly' round Dr. Roylott's head was immediately identified by Holmes. 'It is a swamp adder,' he cried, 'the deadliest snake in India. He has died within ten seconds of being bitten.' But, here again, the zoological critics seem to be in some doubt. The name 'swamp adder' is apparently unknown in their vocabulary and so they have displayed, for our edification, five possible alternatives, including the puff adder and the saw-scaled viper; finally, they give their vote in favour of the cobra. Even so, serious doubt is thrown upon its capacity to kill a man in ten seconds. It is all very disappointing. If we listen to these scientific commentators much longer, we shall be driven to conclude that Holmes himself was guilty of the error that he imputed to Watson—that of tinging what ought to be an exact science with romanticism. There is, however, one zoological exhibit which appears to provoke no controversy, and that is the mounted skin of the giant rat of Sumatra. Here, of course, there is not much to excite biological argument, since our knowledge of the subject is confined to a passing reference. It will be recalled that Holmes's success in the case of Matilda Briggs had made a deep impression on the firm of Morrison, Morrison, and Dodd, and Holmes explained to Watson that Matilda Briggs was the name not of a woman, but of a ship, and that the ship was associated with the giant rat of Sumatra. Here our knowledge ends, since Holmes went on to add that the story was one for which the world was not prepared; but now at least we can see what the giant rat (*Rhizomys Sumatrensis*) was really like. Whether the story was too intimate, or too horrible, for modern ears we can only conjecture. There are several other items in this scientific section, but the fact that the promoters have done nothing about the Devil's Foot (*Radix pedis diaboli*) may be regarded as a curious incident. However, as there was only one sample of it in Europe in 1897 (and that in a laboratory at Buda), we can appreciate the difficulties.

Now let us turn to something more cheerful than poisonous snakes and deadly jelly-fish. One section of the exhibition is devoted to 'Sir Arthur Conan Doyle and the creation of Sherlock Holmes' and perhaps I ought to have begun with this, since after all it was Conan Doyle who, in some magical way, infused the life-blood into his characters. In these days of the immortal youth of his creatures it is well that we should remember the creator, and those who are bibliographically, rather than scientifically, minded can see, for instance, Conan Doyle's first notes for the first Sherlock Holmes story, 'A Study in Scarlet', the story that was refused by several publishers and eventually accepted for inclusion in *Beeton's Christmas Annual* for 1887. This is now a very rare piece and is not shown in the exhibition, but there is a copy of the second edition—also very rare—with illustrations by Charles Doyle, the author's father. First editions of *The Adventures*, *The Memoirs*, *The Hound of the Baskervilles*, and of many other books are also there to be seen and studied.

You can also see one of the stories—'The Adventure of the Dying Detective'—in manuscript. Furthermore, you can study one very important element in the establishment of Holmes and Watson as

living characters—I mean the work of Sidney Paget
as illustrator. If you look up the illustrations in the
first editions of *A Study in Scarlet* and *The Sign of
Four*, you will find both Holmes and Watson to be
quite ludicrously unrecognizable. It was in the *Strand
Magazine* for July 1891, containing 'A Scandal in
Bohemia', that Sidney Paget set the stamp of authenticity upon the physical and sartorial details which are
now permanently associated with the great detective
—the tall, lean figure, the deep-set, piercing eyes,
the deerstalker cap, the travelling cloak, and so on;
and one of the most delightful features of this exhibition is the series of original wash drawings by Sidney
Paget, lent by his daughter, Miss Winifred Paget.
One of them is half of a full-length portrait of Sherlock Holmes which was partially destroyed by the
artist and happily rescued by his wife from the waste-
paper basket; another is the famous drawing entitled
'The Death of Sherlock Holmes', showing Holmes
and Moriarty locked in a deadly embrace on the narrow path above the Reichenbach Falls, and this, by
the way, is supplemented by a photograph of the actual
scene of the struggle, and by a specimen of 'the blackish
soil kept for ever soft by the incessant drift of spray'.

Interest in Sherlock Holmes is not, of course, confined to this country or even to the English-speaking
countries, and copies of various translations are duly
displayed in the exhibition. You can contemplate *La
Vallée de la Peur*, published in Paris in 1920 or *Das
Rätsel der Thor-Brücke und andere Abenteuer*, published

in Berlin in 1928, and there are many other foreign versions whose titles I should be quite unable to enunciate—the *Boscombe Valley Mystery*, for instance, in Danish; *The Hound of the Baskervilles* in Irish, Norwegian, and Polish; other adventures in Arabic, Malay, and Gugarati; and one (*The Six Napoleons*) in Russian. Why the Defence Committee Publishing House of Moscow should have selected the story of the famous black pearl of the Borgias remains a matter for conjecture.

Another section of the exhibition comprises 'Parodies and Cartoons'. One of the earliest parodies was *The Enchanted Typewriter* by J. K. Bangs (1899) and the largest assembly of skits and imitations is contained in *The Misadventures of Sherlock Holmes*, edited by Ellery Queen in 1944. In discussing this particular section I am on slightly delicate ground, since it contains a piece of my own editing—*The Strange Case of the Megatherium Thefts*. This was printed in a very small edition, and for private circulation only, in 1945. At that time, I felt, as Holmes did in another context, that it was a painful story for which the world was not yet prepared. Now, however, that the activities of the principal figure are no longer a prominent scandal, I have thought fit to print the story at the end of this volume.

One of the most attractive parts of the exhibition from the literary point of view is that entitled 'Sherlock Holmes at large'. Here, for instance, it is good to see portraits of the three generations of Vernets, all artists of distinction. Holmes's grandmother was a sister of the third of them, Horace Vernet, and, as I have indicated elsewhere, Holmes may well have been influenced by his great-uncle's picture of his own studio. Here, too, you may get an idea of the ramifications of the intensive study of the Holmes–Watson saga in the last twenty-five years. Foremost in the bibliography of this period stands the famous essay of Monsignor R. A. Knox, entitled 'Studies in the Literature of Sherlock Holmes', which was included in a volume of *Essays in Satire*, published in 1928. It would be impossible to exaggerate the importance of this essay in the history of Holmesian scholarship and my own first contribution to the subject was a review of Monsignor Knox's work.[1] This was followed by a short life of Dr. Watson (1931), which I now observe, with some blushes, to be described as 'the standard biography'.[2] Since 1931 there has been a steady stream of biographical and bibliographical publications, and the work of the late H. W. Bell, of Christopher Morley, T. S. Blakeney, Vincent Starrett, Edgar W. Smith, and many others is well known to all students.

Naturally, this section of the exhibition contains many contributions from across the Atlantic. There the cult of Holmes and Watson has spread to quite astonishing lengths. In 1934 societies to commemorate the name and fame of Sherlock Holmes

---

[1] It should, however, be recorded that as early as 1902 the late Frank Sidgwick called attention in *The Cambridge Review* to a number of chronological inconsistencies in *The Hound of the Baskervilles*.
[2] See p. 61.

were founded both in London and in New York. The moving spirit in the foundation of the London society was the late A. G. Macdonell and I well remember the meeting at which the Society was formed. One point (perhaps the only point) on which we were all agreed was that the society should have a dinner. Where was the dinner to be? 'Surely in Baker Street', I suggested. 'You can't dine in Baker Street', said someone. 'Certainly you can', I replied, and we did dine in Baker Street, hilariously, with the late Dick Sheppard in the chair.

That was in June 1934 and at the same time the society known as the Baker Street Irregulars was founded in New York. The contrast between English casualness and American thoroughness is fully exemplified in the fates of the respective societies. In London two more dinners were held, but after the third dinner members of the society received a laconic postcard: 'The Sherlock Holmes Society, like the Red-Headed League, is dissolved.' In the United States the sequel was very different. Not only have the Baker Street Irregulars survived and expanded, but about thirty scion societies, as they are called, have been formed in various cities of the United States and Canada and one item in the exhibition consists of documents relating to such bodies as the Creeping Men of Cleveland, the Illustrious Clients of Indianapolis, the Six Napoleons of Baltimore, the Trained Cormorants of Los Angeles. It is now pleasant to record that the new Sherlock Holmes Society of London is well established and that two issues of its *Journal* have already appeared.

Another group of miscellaneous items in the exhibition bears the attractive title: 'Is there any other point to which you would wish to draw my attention?'—a quotation, as you will immediately recognize, from *Silver Blaze*. Here there are all sorts of interesting oddments, such as portraits of Holmes in water colour, wood, and poker-work; a rare Sherlock Holmes Crossword Puzzle, by Mycroft Holmes, recently brought to light by Tobias Gregson, late of Scotland Yard, and transmitted by him to Christopher Morley; some highly ingenious reproductions, by the Danish Baker Street Irregulars, of the title-pages of some of Holmes's best-known works, such as 'An Essay on the Polyphonic Motets of Lassus', 'Upon the distinction between the ashes of the various tobaccos', and, of course, of the 'Practical Handbook of Bee Culture, with some observations upon the segregation of the Queen', the *magnum opus* of Holmes's later years.

But most interesting of all the exhibits in this section, perhaps, is the bicycle used by Miss Violet Smith, whose story is told in *The Solitary Cyclist*. According to the managing director of a famous firm of cycle manufacturers, this vehicle was delivered to Miss Smith's father at Charlington Hall in 1895 and after Miss Smith's marriage was sold back to the firm and retained as a period piece. Why Miss Smith, who afterwards inherited a large fortune and became the wife of the senior partner of a famous firm of electricians in Westminster, should have troubled to trade her machine back to the makers is not quite clear. It may be that she merely exchanged it for a later model and the firm has no record of the second transaction; but, in any event, it is pleasant at this distance of time to contemplate the machine and mentally to recall the picture so graphically drawn by Dr. Watson of Miss Violet Smith on her way from Farnham Station: 'In all the broad landscape those were the only moving figures, the graceful girl sitting very straight upon her machine and the man behind her bending low over his handle-bar. . . .'

On the two sections relating to 'Sherlock Holmes on the Stage' and 'Sherlock Holmes on the Screen', I do not feel competent to speak in detail. I did not have the good fortune to see William Gillette in his famous play, but I do recall a certain thrill when I saw the play performed by a good touring company at Cambridge in my undergraduate days. As to Sherlock Holmes on the screen, I cannot help feeling that every sincere devotee of the canonical stories must subscribe to what is said in the Introduction to the catalogue of this section of the exhibition: 'One of the most distressing and inexcusable features of the great majority of the Holmes films is their little resemblance to the stories or characters of the books, for especially in recent times the most appalling perversions of Dr. Watson's immortal narratives have been filmed.' On the other hand, it is pleasant to read and to applaud Lady Conan Doyle's tribute to Mr. Arthur Wontner: 'You looked the part and you seemed the living incarnation of Sherlock.' It is pleasant, too, to note that Mr. Wontner has lent his presentation copy of *The Valley of Fear*, together with the deerstalker and the pipe used by him in the films.

For those who are interested in lethal weapons there is a special section of the exhibition devoted to firearms, and no doubt the revolvers lent by Major Hugh Pollard and others will attract the attention of experts. For myself, I am unable to make any intelligent comment. In the war of 1914–18 I was armed with some sort of revolver and fired some inaccurate shots on a range on the sand-dunes in the neighbourhood of Calais, but I never had occasion to fire it against an enemy. Nor have I ever been tempted to adorn any wall with a V.R., or any other patriotic monogram, in bullet-pocks.

Finally, I come to what is the most alluring part of the exhibition from the point of view of the general public—the reconstruction by Mr. Weight of the living room at No. 221B as it appeared on a foggy evening in 1898. Here is the focus of sentimental reminiscence. The period, of course, is that of the Return of Sherlock Holmes and, as Watson wrote in the story of 'The Empty House', the old landmarks are all in their places. As you lean over a balustrade you look across at a jumble of Victorian, and Sherlockian, bric-à-brac. The ornate overmantel is flanked by two gas brackets; a number of unanswered letters are stuck with a jack-knife into the wood of the mantel-shelf; the Persian slipper is there with tobacco tucked into the toe; on the right is Holmes's chemical corner with its retorts and test-tubes; immediately above it is a snake skin and above that a rack for sticks and riding-crops; by the window is the wax-coloured model of Holmes on the moulding of which Oscar Meunier of Grenoble had expended so much care; on the left of the fireplace are the voluminous and formidable scrapbooks and the pipe-rack; newspapers are lying about on the sofa and elsewhere. Portraits of General Gordon and Henry Ward Beecher recall the blazing hot day in August on which Holmes astonished Watson by reading his train of thought as his eye travelled from one picture to the other.

On the door hangs Watson's top-hat and over it is draped his stethoscope. The pattern of this instrument has been the subject of a lively controversy. Was such a stethoscope in common use amongst practitioners in 1898 or was it not? I regret that I have no opinion to offer on so technical a point. On this or that detail of the reconstruction experts may have criticisms to make, but the total effect remains. Here is the room which, as Mr. Bernard Darwin says in his preface to the catalogue, 'has long since been pictured in the imagination of all the faithful'.

(ii) *Last words*

Why, in conclusion, should it be deemed worth while to make these essays in biographical and topographical reconstruction? The answer is simple: the personalities of Holmes and Watson took such universal hold upon the hearts and imaginations of readers and have retained that hold so tenaciously over a period of sixty years that their lives, their habits, and their characteristics have become an object of greater interest than the adventures which they shared.

'The truth is', wrote Johnson in a highly disputable passage in the Preface to his edition of Shakespeare, 'that the spectators are always in their senses, and know, from the first act to the last, that the stage is only a stage, and that the players are only players.'

Of the drama of Sherlock Holmes the very reverse is the truth. The spectators are not always in their senses and they refuse to treat Holmes and Watson as 'only players'. Conan Doyle, in spite of his own waning interest, created not puppets but characters whom his readers have insisted on regarding as flesh and blood rather than as dramatis personae. Never were two characters more desperately in search of an author than were Holmes and Watson in the years succeeding the tragedy of the Reichenbach Falls; and when *The Empty House*, the story that heralded 'The Return', appeared in the *Strand* for October 1903, the

scenes at railway bookstalls resembled the struggles
in a bargain-basement. One critic remarked that, although Holmes was not killed when he fell over the
cliff, he was never quite the same man afterwards.
But for the common reader it was not the quality of
the later stories that mattered; what mattered was
Holmes's restoration to life, to detective activity, and
to Baker Street. For Holmes returned to a familiar
scene and a beloved companion: 'It was indeed like
old times when, at that hour, I found myself seated
beside him in a hansom, my revolver in my pocket
and the thrill of adventure in my heart.' This was
what Watson felt, and the renewal of the old-time
thrill was communicated to a multitude of readers.
The Baker Street *mise en scène* is indeed one of Conan
Doyle's master-strokes. In some way not easy to
define, No. 221B has become a focal point of the
metropolitan civilization of the 'nineties—the November fogs, the hansoms, the commissionaires, the gasogene, the frock-coats, the Wigmore Street post
office. . . . Many of the adventures contain fantastic
elements and conjure up scenes of distant devilry and
romance; but Holmes and Watson always have their
feet upon the ground. They travel on well-known
railways, they frequent a well-known Turkish bath
establishment, they read the *Daily Telegraph*, they
are in touch with all classes of society. If they are
dealing with members of the middle class (doctors,
solicitors, schoolmasters, engineers, tradesmen) they
are treading on ground familiar to the great mass of

readers; if, on the other hand, they are dealing either with Cabinet Ministers and political dukes or with the crooks and loafers of London's underworld, they give the same readers the thrill that comes with an introduction either to the highest, or to the lowest, strata of society. But, in any event, the reader feels that he is encountering real people, people who do not demand of him any wide exercise of imagination.

In recent years, of course, the public has become familiar with detective stories of vastly more intricate plot, stories of greater complexity and finer ingenuity. Surveying the Sherlock Holmes adventures, the conscientious critic of today would probably give high marks to *Silver Blaze*, for example, or to *The Speckled Band*, but might well think poorly of some of the later stories. 'There are an hundred faults in this Thing', wrote Goldsmith in the Advertisement to *The Vicar of Wakefield*, 'and an hundred things might be said to prove them beauties. But it is needless. A book may be amusing with numerous errors, or it may be very dull without a single absurdity.'

Similarly, it is needless to argue about the faults, or the occasional absurdities, of the Sherlock Holmes stories. From the beginning, a magic seal was set upon them; they were the reminiscences of John H. Watson, M.D., and Watson had the quality which is now regarded as the highest virtue in a broadcaster—he could make his audience feel that he was telling the story from the fireside: ' "My dear fellow", said Sherlock Holmes, as we sat on either side of the fire in his lodgings at Baker Street, "life is infinitely stranger than anything which the mind of man could invent. . . ." '; or ' "Holmes", said I, as I stood one morning in our bow-window looking down the street, "here is a madman coming along. . . ." '; or ' "I am afraid, Watson, that I shall have to go", said Holmes, as we sat down to our breakfast together one morning. "Go! Where to?" "To Dartmoor—to King's Pyland". . . .'

It is this direct, personal introduction that makes the whole scene friendly, intimate, enticing; and at once the reader is agog to hear the details of the latest mystery.

' "Come, Watson, come," cried Holmes, breaking unconsciously on one occasion into a poetical invocation:

'The game is afoot. Not a word!
Into your clothes and come!'

In ten minutes Watson was not only in his clothes, but in a cab, rattling through the streets to Charing Cross Station. There will never be wanting a crowd to follow that cab.

TWO
UNRECORDED
ADVENTURES

TWO UNRECORDED ADVENTURES

(i)

CHRISTMAS EVE

SCENE: The Sitting-room of 221B Baker Street

SHERLOCK HOLMES, *disguised as a loafer, is discovered probing in a sideboard cupboard for something to eat and drink.*

HOLMES. Where in the world is that decanter? I'm sure I——

> *Enter* DR. WATSON, *who sees only the back of Holmes's stooping figure*

WATSON (*turning quickly and whispering hoarsely off stage*). Mrs. Hudson! Mrs. Hudson! My revolver, quick. There's a burglar in Mr. Holmes's room.   [*Exit*

HOLMES. Ah, there's the decanter at last. But first of all I may as well discard some of my properties (*takes off cap, coat, beard, &c, and puts on dressing-gown*). My word, I'm hungry (*begins to eat sandwich*). But, bless me, I've forgotten the gasogene (*stoops at cupboard in same attitude as before*).

> *Enter* WATSON, *followed by* MRS. HUDSON

WATSON (*sternly*). Now, my man, put those hands up.

HOLMES (*turning round*). My dear Watson, why this sudden passion for melodrama?

WATSON. Holmes!

HOLMES. Really, Watson, to be the victim of a murderous

111

attack at your hands, of all people's—and on Christmas Eve, too.

WATSON. But a minute ago, Holmes, there was a villainous-looking scoundrel trying to wrench open that cupboard—a really criminal type. I caught a glimpse of his face.

HOLMES. Well, well, my dear Watson, I suppose I ought to be grateful for the compliment to my make-up (*indicates beard, &c.*). The fact is that I have spent the day loafing at the corner of a narrow street leading out of the Waterloo Road. They were all quite friendly to me there. . . . Yes, I obtained the last little piece of evidence that I wanted to clear up that case of the Kentish Town safe-robbery—you remember? Quite an interesting case, but all over now.

MRS. HUDSON. Lor', Mr. 'Olmes, how you do go on. Still, I'm learnin' never to be surprised at anything now.

HOLMES. Capital, Mrs. Hudson. That's what every criminal investigator has to learn, isn't it Watson?

[*Exit* MRS. HUDSON

WATSON. Well, I suppose so, Holmes. But you must feel very pleased to think you've got that Kentish Town case off your mind before Christmas.

HOLMES. On the contrary, my dear Watson, I'm miserable. I like having things on my mind—it's the only thing that makes life tolerable. A mind empty of problems is worse even than a stomach empty of food (*eats sandwich*). But Christmas is commonly a slack season. I suppose even criminals' hearts are softened. The result is that I have nothing to do but to look out of the window and watch other people being busy. That little pawnbroker at the corner, for instance, you know the one, Watson?

WATSON. Yes, of course.

HOLMES. One of the many shops you have often seen, but never observed, my dear Watson. If you had watched that pawnbroker's front door as carefully as I have during the last ten days, you would have noted a striking increase in his trade; you might have observed also some remarkably well-to-do people going into the shop. There's one well-set-up young woman whom I have seen at least four times. Curious to think what her business may have been. . . . But it's a shame to depress your Christmas spirit, Watson. I see that you are particularly cheerful this morning.

WATSON. Well, yes, I don't mind admitting that I am feeling quite pleased with things today.

HOLMES. So 'Rio Tintos' have paid a good dividend, have they?

WATSON. My dear Holmes, how on earth do you know that?

HOLMES. Elementary, my dear Watson. You told me years ago that 'Rio Tintos' was the one dividend which was paid in through your bank and not direct to yourself. You come into my room with an envelope of a peculiar shade of green sticking out of your coat pocket. That particular shade is used by your bank—Cox's—and by no other, so far as I am aware. Clearly, then, you have just obtained your pass-book from the bank and your cheerfulness must proceed from the good news which it contains. *Ex hypothesi*, that news must relate to 'Rio Tintos'.

WATSON. Perfectly correct, Holmes; and on the strength of the good dividend, I have deposited ten good, crisp, five-pound notes in the drawer of my dressing-table just in case we should feel like a little jaunt after Christmas.

HOLMES. That was charming of you, Watson. But in my present state of inertia I should be a poor holiday-companion. Now if only——(*Knock at door*) Come in.

MRS. HUDSON. Please sir, there's a young lady to see you.

HOLMES. What sort of young lady, Mrs. Hudson? Another of these young women wanting half a crown towards some Christmas charity? If so, Dr. Watson's your man, Mrs. Hudson. He's bursting with bank-notes this morning.

MRS. HUDSON. I'm sure I'm very pleased to 'ear it, sir; but this lady ain't that kind at all, sir. She's sort of agitated, like . . . very anxious to see you and quite scared of meeting you at the same time, if you take my meaning, sir.

HOLMES. Perfectly, Mrs. Hudson. Well, Watson, what are we to do? Are we to interview this somewhat unbalanced young lady?

WATSON. If the poor girl is in trouble, Holmes, I think you might at least hear what she has to say.

HOLMES. Chivalrous as ever, my dear Watson—Bring the lady up, Mrs. Hudson.

MRS. HUDSON. Very good, sir. (*To the lady outside*) This way, Miss.

Enter MISS VIOLET DE VINNE, *an elegant but distracted girl of about twenty-two*

HOLMES (*bowing slightly*). You wish to consult me?

MISS DE VINNE (*nervously*). Are you Mr. Sherlock Holmes?

HOLMES. I am—and this is my friend and colleague, Dr. Watson.

WATSON (*coming forward and holding out hand*). Charmed, I am sure, Miss——

HOLMES (*to* MISS DE VINNE). You have come here, I presume, because you have a story to tell me. May I ask you to be as concise as possible?

MISS DE VINNE. I will try, Mr. Holmes. My name is de Vinne. My mother and I live together in Bayswater. We are not very well off, but my father was . . . well . . . a gentleman. The Countess of Barton is one of our oldest friends——

HOLMES (*interrupting*). And the owner of a very wonderful pearl necklace.

MISS DE VINNE (*startled*). How do you know that, Mr. Holmes?

HOLMES. I am afraid it is my business to know quite a lot about other people's affairs. But I'm sorry. I interrupted. Go on.

MISS DE VINNE. Two or three times a week I spend the day with Lady Barton and act as her secretary in a casual, friendly way. I write letters for her and arrange her dinner-tables when she has a party and do other little odd jobs.

HOLMES. Lady Barton is fortunate, eh, Watson?

WATSON. Yes, indeed, Holmes.

MISS DE VINNE. This afternoon a terrible thing happened. I was arranging some flowers when Lady Barton came in looking deathly white. 'Violet,' she said, 'the pearls have gone.' 'Heavens,' I cried, 'what do you mean?' 'Well,' she said, 'having quite unexpectedly had an invitation to a reception on January 5th, I thought I would make sure that the clasp was all right. When I opened the case (you know the special place where I keep it) it was empty—that's all.' She looked as if she was going to faint, and I felt much the same.

HOLMES (*quickly*). And did you faint?

MISS DE VINNE. N o, Mr. Holmes, we pulled ourselve together somehow and I asked her whether she was going to send for the police, but she wouldn't hear of it. She said Jim (that's her husband) hated publicity and would be furious if the pearls became 'copy' for journalists. But of course she agreed that something had to be done and so she sent me to you.

HOLMES. Oh, Lady Barton sent you?

MISS DE VINNE. Well, not exactly. You see, when she refused to send for the police, I remembered your name and implored her to write to you . . . and . . . well . . . here I am and here's the letter. That's all, Mr. Holmes.

HOLMES. I see (*begins to read letter*). Well, my dear lady, neither you nor Lady Barton has given me much material on which to work at present.

MISS DE VINNE. I am willing to answer any questions, Mr. Holmes.

HOLMES. You live in Bayswater, Miss Winnie?

WATSON (*whispering*). 'De Vinne', Holmes.

HOLMES (*ignoring* WATSON). You said Bayswater, I think, Miss Winnie?

MISS DE VINNE. Quite right, Mr. Holmes, but—forgive me, my name is De Vinne.

HOLMES. I'm sorry, Miss Dwinney——

MISS DE VINNE. DE VINNE, Mr. Holmes, D . . . E . . . V. . . .

HOLMES. How stupid of me. I think the chill I caught last week must have left a little deafness behind it. But to save further stupidity on my part, just write your name and address for me, will you? (*Hands her pen and paper, on which* MISS DE VINNE *writes*) That's better. Now, tell me, Miss de Vinne, how do you find Bayswater for shopping?

MISS DE VINNE (*surprised*). Oh, I don't know. Mr. Holmes, I hardly——

HOLMES. You don't care for Whiteley's, for instance?

MISS DE VINNE. Well, not very much. But I can't see . . .

HOLMES. I entirely agree with you, Miss de Vinne. Yet Watson, you know, is devoted to that place—spends hours there . . .

WATSON. Holmes, what nonsense are you——

HOLMES. But I think you are quite right, Miss de Vinne. Harrod's is a great deal better in my opinion.

MISS DE VINNE. But I never go to Harrod's, Mr. Holmes, in fact I hardly ever go to any big store, except for one or two things. But what has this got to do——

HOLMES. Well, in principle, I don't care for them much either, but they're convenient sometimes.

MISS DE VINNE. Yes, I find the Army and Navy stores useful now and then, but why on earth are we talking about shops and stores when the thing that matters is Lady Barton's necklace?

HOLMES. Ah, yes, I was coming to that (*pauses*). I'm sorry, Miss de Vinne, but I'm afraid I can't take up this case.

MISS DE VINNE. You refuse, Mr. Holmes?

HOLMES. I am afraid I am obliged to do so. It is a case that would inevitably take some time. I am in sore need of a holiday and only today my devoted friend Watson has made all arrangements to take me on a Mediterranean cruise immediately after Christmas.

WATSON. Holmes, this is absurd. You know that I merely——

MISS DE VINNE. Doctor Watson, if Mr. Holmes can't help me, won't you? You don't know how terrible all this is for me as well as for Lady Barton.

WATSON. My dear lady, I have some knowledge of my friend's methods and they often seem incomprehensible. (*To* HOLMES) Holmes, you can't mean this?

HOLMES. Certainly I do, my dear Watson. But I am unwilling that any lady should leave this house in a state of distress. (*Goes to door*) Mrs. Hudson!

MRS. HUDSON. Coming, sir. [*Enters*

HOLMES. Mrs. Hudson, be good enough to conduct this lady to Dr. Watson's dressing-room. She is tired and a little upset. Let her rest on the sofa there while Dr. Watson and I have a few minutes' quiet talk.

MRS. HUDSON. Very good, sir.

[*Exeunt* MRS. HUDSON *and* MISS DE VINNE,
the latter looking appealingly at DR. WATSON

HOLMES (*lighting cherry-wood pipe*). Well, Watson?

WATSON. Well, Holmes, in all my experience I don't think I have ever seen you so unaccountably ungracious to a charming girl.

HOLMES. Oh, yes, she has charm, Watson—they always have. What do you make of her story?

WATSON. Not very much, I confess. It seemed fairly clear as far as it went, but you wouldn't let her tell us any detail. Instead, you began a perfectly ridiculous conversation about the comparative merits of various department stores. I've seldom heard you so inept.

HOLMES. Then you accept her story?

WATSON. Why not?

HOLMES. Why not, my dear Watson? Because the whole thing is a parcel of lies.

WATSON. But, Holmes, this is unreasoning prejudice.

HOLMES. Unreasoning, you say? Listen, Watson. This letter purports to have come from the Countess of Barton. I don't know her ladyship's handwriting, but I was struck at once by its laboured character, as exhibited in this note. It occurred to me, further, that it might be useful to obtain a specimen of Miss de Vinne's to put alongside it—hence my tiresome inability to catch her name. Now, my dear Watson, I call your particular attention to the capital B's which happen to occur in both specimens.

WATSON. They're quite different, Holmes, but—yes, they've both got a peculiar curl where the letter finishes.

HOLMES. Point number one, my dear Watson, but an isolated one. Now, although I could not recognize the handwriting, I knew this note-paper as soon as I saw and felt it. Look at the watermark, Watson, and tell me what you find.

WATSON (*holding the paper to the light*). A. and N. . . . . (*after a pause*) Army and Navy. . . . Why, Holmes, d'you mean that——

HOLMES. I mean that this letter was written by your charming friend in the name of the Countess of Barton.

WATSON. And what follows?

HOLMES. Ah, that is what we are left to conjecture. What will follow immediately is another interview with the young woman who calls herself Violet de Vinne. By the way, Watson, after you had finished threatening me with that nasty-looking revolver a little while ago, what did you do with the instrument?

WATSON. It's here, Holmes, in my pocket.

HOLMES. Then, having left my own in my bed-room, I think I'll borrow it, if you don't mind.

WATSON. But surely Holmes, you don't suggest that——

HOLMES. My dear Watson, I suggest nothing—except that we may possibly find ourselves in rather deeper waters than Miss de Vinne's charm and innocence have hitherto led you to expect. (*Goes to door*) Mrs. Hudson, ask the lady to be good enough to rejoin us.

MRS. HUDSON (*off*). Very good, sir.

Enter MISS DE VINNE

HOLMES (*amiably*). Well, Miss de Vinne, are you rested?

MISS DE VINNE. Well, a little perhaps, but as you can do nothing for me, hadn't I better go?

HOLMES. You look a little flushed, Miss de Vinne; do you feel the room rather too warm?

MISS DE VINNE. No, Mr. Holmes, thank you, I——

HOLMES. Anyhow, won't you slip your coat off and——

MISS DE VINNE. Oh no, really (*gathers coat round her*).

HOLMES (*threateningly*). Then, if you won't take your coat off (*getting up from chair*) d'you mind showing me what is in the right-hand pocket of it? (*A look of terror comes on* MISS DE VINNE's *face*) The game's up, Violet de Vinne (*points revolver, at which* MISS DE VINNE *screams and throws up her hands*). Watson, oblige me by removing whatever you may discover in the right-hand pocket of Miss de Vinne's coat.

WATSON (*taking out note-case*). My own note-case, Holmes, with the ten five-pound notes in it!

HOLMES. Ah!

MISS DE VINNE (*distractedly*). Let me speak, let me speak. I'll explain everything.

HOLMES. Silence! Watson, was there anything else in the drawer of your dressing-table besides your note-case?

WATSON. I'm not sure, Holmes.

HOLMES. Then I think we had better have some verification.

MISS DE VINNE. No, no, let me——

HOLMES. Mrs. Hudson!

MRS. HUDSON (*off*). Coming, sir.

HOLMES (*to* MRS. HUDSON *off*). Kindly open the right-hand drawer of Dr. Watson's dressing-table and bring us anything that you may find in it.

MISS DE VINNE. Mr. Holmes, you are torturing me. Let me tell you everything.

HOLMES. Your opportunity will come in due course, but in all probability before a different tribunal. I am a private detective, not a Criminal Court judge. (MISS DE VINNE *weeps.*)

Enter MRS. HUDSON *with jewel case*

MRS. HUDSON. I found this, sir. But it must be something new that the doctor's been buying. I've never seen it before.　　　　　　　　　　　　　　　　　　　[*Exit*

HOLMES. Ah, Watson, more surprises (*opens case and holds up a string of pearls*). The famous pearls belonging to the Countess of Barton, if I mistake not.

MISS DE VINNE. For pity's sake, Mr. Holmes, let me speak. Even the lowest criminal has that right left him. And this time I will tell you the truth.

HOLMES (*sceptically*). The truth? Well?

MISS DE VINNE. Mr. Holmes, I have an only brother. He's a dear—I love him better than anyone in the world—but, God forgive him, he's a scamp . . . always in trouble, always in debt. Three days ago he wrote to me that he was in an even deeper hole than usual. If he couldn't raise fifty pounds in the course of a week, he would be done for and, worse than that, dishonoured and disgraced for ever. I couldn't bear it. I'd no money. I daren't tell my mother. I swore to myself that I'd get that fifty pounds if I had to steal it. That same day at Lady Barton's, I was looking, as I'd often looked, at the famous pearls. An idea suddenly came to me. They were worn only once or twice a year on special occasions. Why shouldn't I pawn them for a month or so? I could surely get fifty pounds for them and then somehow I would scrape together the money to redeem them. It was almost certain that Lady Barton wouldn't want them for six months. Oh, I know I was mad, but I did it. I found a fairly obscure little pawnbroker quite near here, but to my horror he wouldn't take the pearls—looked at me very suspiciously and wouldn't budge, though I went to him two or three times. Then, this afternoon, the crash came. When Lady Barton discovered that the pearls were missing I rushed out of the house, saying that I would tell the police. But actually I went home and tried to think. I remembered your name. A wild scheme came into my head. If I could pretend to consult you and somehow leave the pearls in your house, then you could pretend that you had recovered them and return them to Lady Barton. Oh, I know you'll laugh, but you don't know how distraught I was. Then, when you sent me into that dressing-room, I prowled about like a caged animal. I saw those banknotes and they seemed like a gift from Heaven. Why shouldn't I leave the necklace in their place? You would get much more than fifty pounds for recovering them from Lady Barton and I should save my brother. There, that's all . . . and now, I suppose, I exchange Dr. Watson's dressing-room for a cell at the police station!

HOLMES. Well, Watson?

WATSON. What an extraordinary story, Holmes.

HOLMES. Yes, indeed. (*Turning to* MISS DE VINNE) Miss de Vinne, you told us in the first instance a plausible story of which I did not believe a single word; now you have given us a version which in many particulars seems absurd and incredible. Yet I believe it to be the truth. (*To* WATSON) Watson, haven't I always told you that fact is immeasurably stranger than fiction?

WATSON. Certainly, Holmes. But what are you going to do?

HOLMES. Going to do? Why——er——I'm going to send for Mrs. Hudson. (*Calling off stage*) Mrs. Hudson.

MRS. HUDSON (*off*). Coming, sir (*enters*). Yes, sir.

HOLMES. Oh, Mrs. Hudson, what are your views about Christmas?

WATSON. Really, Holmes.

HOLMES. My dear Watson, please don't interrupt. As I was saying, Mrs. Hudson, I should be very much interested to know how you feel about Christmas.

MRS. HUDSON. Lor', Mr. 'Olmes, what questions you do ask. I don't 'ardly know exactly how to answer but . . . well . . . I suppose Christmas is the season of good-will towards men—and women too, sir, if I may say so.

HOLMES (*slowly*). 'And women too.' You observe that, Watson.

WATSON. Yes, Holmes, and I agree.

HOLMES (*to* MISS DE VINNE). My dear young lady, you will observe that the jury are agreed upon their verdict.

MISS DE VINNE. Oh, Mr. Holmes, how can I ever thank you?

HOLMES. Not a word. You must thank the members of the jury. . . . Mrs. Hudson!

MRS. HUDSON. Yes, sir.

HOLMES. Take Miss de Vinne, not into Dr. Watson's room this time, but into your own comfortable kitchen and give her a cup of your famous tea.

MRS. HUDSON. How do the young lady take it, sir? Rather strong like, with a bit of a tang to it?

HOLMES. You must ask her that yourself. Anyhow Mrs. Hudson, give her the cup that cheers.

[*Exeunt* MRS. HUDSON *and* MISS DE VINNE

WATSON (*in the highest spirits*). Half a minute, Mrs. Hudson. I'm coming to see that Miss de Vinne has her tea as she likes it. And I tell you what, Holmes, (*looking towards* MISS DE VINNE *and holding up note-case*) you are not going to get your Mediterranean cruise. [*Exit*

As WATSON *goes out, carol-singers are heard in the distance singing* Good King Wenceslas

HOLMES (*relighting his pipe and smiling meditatively*). Christmas Eve!

CURTAIN

THE STRANGE CASE OF THE MEGATHERIUM THEFTS

I have already had occasion, in the course of these reminiscences of my friend Sherlock Holmes, to refer to his liking for the Diogenes Club, the club which contained the most unsociable men in London and forbade talking save in the Strangers' Room. So far as I am aware, this was the only club to which Holmes was attracted, and it struck me as not a little curious that he should have been called upon to solve the extraordinary mystery of the Megatherium Thefts.

It was a dull afternoon in November and Holmes, turning wearily from the cross-indexing of some old newspaper-cuttings, drew his chair near to mine and took out his watch.

'How slow life has become, my dear Watson,' he said, 'since the successful conclusion of that little episode in a lonely west-country village. Here we are back amongst London's millions and nobody wants us.'

He crossed to the window, opened it a little, and peered through the November gloom into Baker Street.

'No, Watson, I'm wrong. I believe we are to have a visitor.'

'Is there someone at the door?'

'Not yet. But a hansom has stopped opposite to it. The passenger has alighted and there is a heated discussion in progress concerning the fare. I cannot hear the argument in detail, but it is a lively one.'

A few minutes later the visitor was shown into the sitting-room—a tall, stooping figure with a straggling white beard, shabbily dressed and generally unkempt. He spoke with a slight stutter.

'M-Mr. Sherlock Holmes?' he inquired.

'That is my name,' replied Holmes, 'and this is my friend, Dr. Watson.'

The visitor bowed jerkily and Holmes continued: 'And whom have I the honour of addressing?'

'My n-name is Wiskerton—Professor Wiskerton—and I have ventured to call upon you in connexion with a most remarkable and puzzling affair.'

'We are familiar with puzzles in this room, Professor.'

'Ah, but not with any like this one. You see, apart from my p-professorial standing, I am one of the oldest members of——'

'The Megatherium?'

'My dear sir, how did you know?'

'Oh, there was no puzzle about that. I happened to hear some reference in your talk with the cabman to your journey having begun at Waterloo Place. Clearly you had travelled from one of two clubs and somehow I should not associate you with the United Services.'

'You're p-perfectly right, of course. The driver of that cab was a rapacious scoundrel. It's s-scandalous that——'

'But you have not come to consult me about an extortionate cab-driver?'

'No, no. Of course not. It's about——'

'The Megatherium?'

'Exactly. You see, I am one of the oldest m-members and have been on the Committee for some years. I need hardly tell you the kind of standing which the Megatherium has in the world of learning, Mr. Holmes.'

'Dr. Watson, I have no doubt, regards the institution with veneration. For myself, I prefer the soothing atmosphere of the Diogenes.'

'The w-what?'

'The Diogenes Club.'

'N-never heard of it.'

'Precisely. It is a club of which people are not meant to hear—but I beg your pardon for this digression. You were going to say?'

'I was g-going to say that the most distressing thing has happened. I should explain in the first place that in addition to the n-noble collection of books in the Megatherium library, a collection which is one of our most valuable assets, we have available at any one time a number of books from one of the circulating libraries and——'

'And you are losing them?'

'Well—yes, in fact we are. But how did you know?'

'I didn't know—I merely made a deduction. When a client begins to describe his possessions to me, it is generally because some misfortune has occurred in connexion with them.'

'But this is m-more than a m-misfortune, Mr. Holmes. It is a disgrace, an outrage, a——'

'But what, in fact, has happened?'

'Ah, I was c-coming to that. But perhaps it would be simpler if I showed you this document and let it speak for itself. P-personally, I think it was a mistake to circulate it, but the Committee over-ruled me and now the story will be all over London and we shall still be no nearer a solution.'

Professor Wiskerton fumbled in his pocket and produced a printed document marked *Private and Confidential* in bold red type.

'What do you m-make of it, Mr. Holmes? Isn't it extraordinary? Here is a club whose members are selected from among the most distinguished representatives of the arts and sciences and this is the way they treat the c-club property.'

Holmes paid no attention to the Professor's rambling commentary and continued his reading of the document.

'You have brought me quite an interesting case, Professor', he said, at length.

'But it is more than interesting, Mr. Holmes. It is astonishing. It is inexplicable.'

'If it were capable of easy explanation, it would cease to be interesting and, furthermore, you would not have spent the money on a cab-fare to visit me.'

'That, I suppose, is true. But what do you advise, Mr. Holmes?'

'You must give me a little time, Professor. Perhaps you will be good enough to answer one or two questions first?'

'Willingly.'

'This document states that your Committee is satisfied that no member of the staff is implicated. You are satisfied yourself on that point?'

'I am not s-satisfied about anything, Mr. Holmes. As one who has s-spent a great part of his life amongst books and libraries, the whole subject of the maltreatment of books is repugnant to me. Books are my life-blood, Mr. Holmes. But perhaps I have not your s-sympathy?'

'On the contrary, Professor, I have a genuine interest in such matters. For myself, however, I travel in those by-ways of bibliophily which are associated with my own profession.'

Holmes moved across to a shelf and took out a volume with which I had long been familiar.

'Here, Professor,' he continued, 'if I may rid myself of false modesty for the moment, is a little monograph of mine *Upon the Distinction Between the Ashes of the Various Tobaccos.*'

'Ah, most interesting, Mr. Holmes. Not being a smoker myself, I cannot pretend to appraise your work from the point of view of scholarship, but as a bibliophile and especially as a c-collector of out-of-the-way monographs, may I ask whether the work is still available?'

'That is a spare copy, Professor; you are welcome to it.'

The Professor's eyes gleamed with voracious pleasure.

'But, Mr. Holmes, this is m-most generous of you. May I b-beg that you will inscribe it? I derive a special delight from what are called "association copies".'

'Certainly', said Holmes, with a smile, as he moved to the writing-table.

'Thank you, thank you,' murmured the Professor, 'but I fear I have distracted you from the main issue.'

'Not at all.'

'But what is your p-plan, Mr. Holmes? Perhaps you would like to have a look round the Megatherium? Would you care, for instance, to have luncheon to-morrow—but no, I fear I am engaged at that time. What about a c-cup of tea at 4 o'clock?'

'With pleasure. I trust I may bring Dr. Watson, whose co-operation in such cases has frequently been of great value?'

'Oh-er-yes, certainly.'

But it did not seem to me that there was much cordiality in his assent.

'Very well, then,' said Holmes. 'The document which you have left with me gives the facts and I will study them with great care.'

'Thank you, thank you. To-morrow, then, at 4 o'clock,' said the Professor, as he shook hands, 'and I shall t-treasure this volume, Mr. Holmes.'

He slipped the monograph into a pocket and left us.

'Well, Watson,' said Holmes, as he filled his pipe, 'What do you make of this curious little case?'

'Very little, at present. I haven't had a chance to examine the *data*.'

'Quite right, Watson. I will reveal them to you.' Holmes took up the sheet which the Professor had left.

'This is a confidential letter circulated to members of the Megatherium and dated November 1889. I'll read you a few extracts:

"In a recent report the Committee drew attention to the serious loss and inconvenience caused by the removal from the Club of books from the circulating library. The practice has continued. . . . At the end of June, the Club paid for no less than 22 missing volumes. By the end of September 15 more were missing. . . . The Committee were disposed to ascribe these malpractices to some undetected individual member, but they have regretfully come to the conclusion that more members than one are involved. They are fully satisfied that no member of the staff is in any way implicated. . . . If the offenders can be identified, the Committee will not hesitate to apply the Rule which empowers expulsion."

There, Watson, what do you think of that?'

'Most extraordinary, Holmes—at the Megatherium, of all clubs.'

'*Corruptio optimi pessima*, my dear Watson.'

'D'you think the Committee is right about the servants?'

'I'm not interested in the Committee's opinions, Watson, even though they be the opinions of Bishops and Judges and Fellows of the Royal Society. I am concerned only with the facts.'

'But the facts are simple, Holmes. Books are being stolen in considerable quantities from the club and the thief, or thieves, have not been traced.'

'Admirably succinct, my dear Watson. And the motive?'

'The thief's usual motive, I suppose—the lure of illicit gain.'

'But what gain, Watson? If you took half a dozen books,

with the mark of a circulating library on them, to a second-hand bookseller, how much would you expect to get for them?'

'Very little, certainly, Holmes.'

'Yes, and that is why the Committee is probably right in ruling out the servants—not that I believe in ruling out anybody or anything on *a priori* grounds. But the motive of gain won't do. You must try again, Watson.'

'Well, of course, people are careless about books, especially when they belong to someone else. Isn't it possible that members take these books away from the club, intending to return them, and then leave them in the train or mislay them at home?'

'Not bad, my dear Watson, and a perfectly reasonable solution if we were dealing with a loss of three or four volumes. In that event our Professor would probably not have troubled to enlist my humble services. But look at the figures, Watson—twenty-two books missing in June, fifteen more in September. There's something more than casual forgetfulness in that.'

'That's true, Holmes, and I suppose we can't discover much before we keep our appointment at the Megatherium tomorrow.'

'On the contrary, my dear Watson, I hope to pursue a little independent investigation this evening.'

'I should be delighted to accompany you, Holmes.'

'I am sure you would, Watson, but if you will forgive me for saying so, the little inquiry I have to make is of a personal nature and I think it might be more fruitful if I were alone.'

'Oh, very well,' I replied, a little nettled at Holmes's superior manner, 'I can employ myself very profitably in reading this new work on surgical technique which has just come to hand.'

I saw little of Holmes on the following morning. He

made no reference to the Megatherium case at breakfast and disappeared shortly afterwards. At luncheon he was in high spirits. There was a gleam in his eye which showed me that he was happily on the trail.

'Holmes,' I said, 'you have discovered something.'

'My dear Watson,' he replied, 'your acuteness does you credit. I have discovered that after an active morning I am extremely hungry.'

But I was not to be put off.

'Come, Holmes, I am too old a campaigner to be bluffed in that way. How far have you penetrated into the Megatherium mystery?'

'Far enough to make me look forward to our tea-party with a lively interest.'

Being familiar with my friend's bantering manner, I recognized that it was no good pressing him with further questions for the moment.

Shortly after 4 o'clock Holmes and I presented ourselves at the portals of the Megatherium. The head porter received us very courteously and seemed, I thought, almost to recognize Sherlock Holmes. He conducted us to a seat in the entrance-hall and, as soon as our host appeared, we made our way up the noble staircase to the long drawing-room on the first floor.

'Now let me order some tea,' said the Professor. 'Do you like anything to eat with it, Mr. Holmes?'

'Just a biscuit for me, Professor, but my friend Watson has an enormous appetite.'

'Really, Holmes——' I began.

'No, no. Just a little pleasantry of mine,' said Holmes, quickly. I thought I observed an expression of relief on the Professor's face.

'Well, now, about our p-problem, Mr. Holmes. Is there any further information that I can give you?'

'I should like to have a list of the titles of the books which have most recently disappeared.'

'Certainly, Mr. Holmes, I can get that for you at once.'

The Professor left us for a few minutes and returned with a paper in his hand. I looked over Holmes's shoulder while he read and recognized several well-known books that had been recently published, such as *Robbery under Arms*, *Troy Town*, *The Economic Interpretation of History*, *The Wrong Box*, and *Three Men in a Boat*.

'Do you make any particular deductions from the titles, Mr. Holmes?' the Professor asked.

'I think not,' Holmes replied; 'there are, of course, certain very popular works of fiction, some other books of more general interest and a few titles of minor importance. I do not think one could draw any conclusion about the culprit's special sphere of interest.'

'You think not? Well, I agree, Mr. Holmes. It is all very b-baffling.'

'Ah,' said Holmes suddenly, 'this title reminds me of something.'

'What is that, Mr. Holmes?'

'I see that one of the missing books is *Plain Tales from the Hills*. It happens that I saw an exceptionally interesting copy of that book not long ago. It was an advance copy, specially bound and inscribed for presentation to the author's godson who was sailing for India before the date of publication.'

'Really, Mr. Holmes, really? That is of the greatest interest to me.'

'Your own collection, Professor, is, I suspect, rich in items of such a kind?'

'Well, well, it is not for me to b-boast, Mr. Holmes, but I certainly have one or two volumes of unique association value on my shelves. I am a poor man and do not aspire to first folios, but the p-pride of my collection is that it could not have been assembled through the ordinary channels of trade. . . . But to return to our problem, is there anything else in the Club which you would like to investigate?'

'I think not,' said Holmes, 'but I must confess that the description of your collection has whetted my own bibliographical appetite.'

The Professor flushed with pride.

'Well, Mr. Holmes, if you and your friend would really care to see my few t-treasures, I should be honoured. My rooms are not f-far from here.'

'Then let us go,' said Holmes, with decision.

I confess that I was somewhat puzzled by my friend's behaviour. He seemed to have forgotten the misfortunes of the Megatherium and to be taking a wholly disproportionate interest in the eccentricities of the Wiskerton collection.

When we reached the Professor's rooms I had a further surprise. I had expected not luxury, of course, but at least some measure of elegance and comfort. Instead, the chairs and tables, the carpets and curtains, everything, in fact, seemed to be of the cheapest quality; even the bookshelves were of plain deal and roughly put together. The books themselves were another matter. They were classified like no other library I had ever seen. In one section were presentation copies from authors; in another were proof-copies bound in what is known as 'binder's cloth'; in another were review copies; in another were pamphlets, monographs, and off-prints of all kinds.

'There you are, Mr. Holmes,' said the Professor, with all the pride of ownership. 'You may think it is a c-collection of oddities, but for me every one of those volumes has a p-personal and s-separate association—including the item which came into my hands yesterday afternoon.'

'Quite so,' said Holmes, thoughtfully, 'and yet they all have a common characteristic.'

'I don't understand you.'

'No? But I am waiting to see the remainder of your collection, Professor. When I have seen the whole of your library, I shall perhaps be able to explain myself more clearly.'

The Professor flushed with annoyance.

'Really, Mr. Holmes, I had been warned of some of your p-peculiarities of manner; but I am entirely at a loss to know what you are d-driving at.'

'In that case, Professor, I will thank you for your hospitality and will beg leave to return to the Megatherium for consultation with the Secretary.'

'To tell him that you can't f-find the missing books?'

Sherlock Holmes said nothing for a moment. Then he looked straight into the Professor's face and said, very slowly:

'On the contrary, Professor Wiskerton, I shall tell the Secretary that I can direct him to the precise address at which the books may be found.'

There was silence. Then an extraordinary thing happened.

The Professor turned away and literally crumpled into a chair; then he looked up at Holmes with the expression of a terrified child:

'Don't do it, Mr. Holmes. Don't do it, I b-b-beseech you. I'll t-tell you everything.'

'Where are the books?' asked Holmes, sternly.

'Come with me and I'll show you.'

The Professor shuffled out and led us into a dismal bedroom. With a trembling hand he felt in his pocket for his keys and opened a cupboard alongside the wall. Several rows of books were revealed and I quickly recognized one or two titles that I had seen on the Megatherium list.

'Oh, what m-must you think of me, Mr. Holmes?' the Professor began, whimpering.

'My opinion is irrelevant,' said Sherlock Holmes, sharply. 'Have you any packing-cases?'

'No, but I d-daresay my landlord might be able to find some.'

'Send for him.'

In a few minutes the landlord appeared. Yes, he thought he could find a sufficient number of cases to take the books in the cupboard.

'Professor Wiskerton,' said Holmes, 'is anxious to have all these books packed at once and sent to the Megatherium, Pall Mall. The matter is urgent.'

'Very good, sir. Any letter or message to go with them?'

'No,' said Holmes, curtly, 'but yes—stop a minute.'

He took a pencil and a visiting-card from his pocket and wrote 'With the compliments of' above the name.

'See that this card is firmly attached to the first of the packing-cases. Is that clear?'

'Quite correct, sir, if that's what the Professor wants.'

'That is what the Professor most particularly wants. Is it not, Professor?' said Holmes, with great emphasis.

'Yes, yes, I suppose so. But c-come back with me into the other room and l-let me explain.'

We returned to the sitting-room and the Professor began:

'Doubtless I seem to you either ridiculous or despicable or both. I have had two p-passions in my life—a passion for s-saving money and a passion for acquiring b-books. As a result of an unfortunate dispute with the Dean of my faculty at the University, I retired at a c-comparatively early age and on a very small p-pension. I was determined to amass a collection of books; I was equally determined not to s-spend my precious savings on them. The idea came to me that my library should be unique, in that all the books in it should be acquired by some means other than p-purchase. I had friends amongst authors, printers, and publishers, and I did pretty well, but there were many recently published books that I wanted and saw no m-means of getting until—well, until I absent-mindedly brought home one of the circulating library books from the Megatherium. I meant to return it, of course. But I didn't. Instead, I b-brought home another one. . . .'

'*Facilis descensus* . . .,' murmured Holmes.

'Exactly, Mr. Holmes, exactly. Then, when the Committee began to notice that books were disappearing, I was in a quandary. But I remembered hearing someone say in another connexion that the b-best defence was attack and I thought that if I were the first to go to you, I should be the last to be s-suspected.'

'I see,' said Holmes. 'Thank you, Professor Wiskerton.'

'And now what are you going to do?'

'First', replied Holmes, 'I am going to make certain that your landlord has those cases ready for despatch. After that, Dr. Watson and I have an engagement at St. James's Hall.'

'A trivial little case, Watson, but not wholly without interest,' said Holmes, when we returned from the concert hall to Baker Street.

'A most contemptible case, in my opinion. Did you guess from the first that Wiskerton himself was the thief?'

'Not quite, Watson. I never guess. I endeavour to observe. And the first thing I observed about Professor Wiskerton was that he was a miser—the altercation with the cabman, the shabby clothes, the unwillingness to invite us to lunch. That he was an enthusiastic bibliophile was,

of course, obvious. At first I was not quite certain how to
fit these two characteristics properly together, but after.
yesterday's interview I remembered that the head porter
of the Megatherium had been a useful ally of mine in his
earlier days as a Commissionaire and I thought a private
talk with him might be useful. His brief characterization
put me on the right track at once—"Always here reading",
he said, "but never takes a square meal in the club." After
that, and after a little hasty research this morning into the
Professor's academic career, I had little doubt.'

'But don't you still think it extraordinary, in spite of
what he said, that he should have taken the risk of coming
to consult you?'

'Of course it's extraordinary, Watson. Wiskerton's an
extraordinary man. If, as I hope, he has the decency to
resign from the Megatherium, I shall suggest to Mycroft
that he puts him up for the Diogenes.'